HMS HOOD - FAME AND MISFORTUNE

The Loss of HMS Hood during the Battle of the Denmark Strait

By Phil Trigg

North
Staffordshire
Press

**North Staffordshire Press
Newcastle-under-Lyme
Staffordshire**

i

HMS Hood – Fame and Misfortune

ISBN 978-0-9935783-7-3

First Published in 2017
By
North Staffordshire Press
Brampton Business Centre
10 Queen Street
Newcastle-under-Lyme
ST5 1ED

To the late Jim Murray: an old sea-dog, model-maker
and kindred spirit.

Acknowledgements

This work is the outcome of a long-standing interest in the twenty one year life, and sudden death, of the battlecruiser HMS Hood. Some memorable steps along the way have included my first reading of "The Mighty Hood" by Ernle Bradford, viewing the film "Sink the Bismarck" and admiring the enormous skill embodied in "Anatomy of the Ship: Battlecruiser Hood" by John Roberts. Also worthy of mention - as recounted in the book "Flagship Hood" - are the narrow escape and subsequent rescue of Ted Briggs and two other survivors. Some of my material was prepared while taking part in a stimulating Channel 4 web forum, linked with the search for the ship's final resting place in the Denmark Strait.

Battlecruiser Hood and battleship Bismarck are the main "characters" in the following narrative. However, they were part of a greater drama of naval rivalry and fighting at sea in two world wars. The times and the passions have passed into history, but it is fitting that many other fine ships, and the brave men who served in them, should be remembered within these pages.

Some impressive works of research and scholarship were uncovered as I went through the convoluted writing processes. I am grateful to those who agreed to my making specific use of their published material.

Several friends should also be mentioned for their encouragement and support in bringing this work to completion. Thanks go to Peter Colmans, Roger Dawe, Chris Gazzard, Sally Hunt, Sean Ryan, Roger Turner - and Malcolm Henson from North Staffordshire Press.

Aims of this Work

1. *To trace the origins and development of HMS Hood, amongst British battlecruisers and battleships of the dreadnought era.*
2. *To outline the changing fortunes of the British battlecruiser as a type of ship, with reference to the battle of Jutland (31 May 1916).*
3. *To provide a narrative on the interception of a German raiding squadron in the Denmark Strait (24 May 1941).*
4. *To describe the deployment and loss of HMS Hood during that encounter.*
5. *To examine and comment on a number of issues arising, including whether there may have been an 'immune zone' for the ship, within which her part of the engagement could have been fought.*
6. *To apply basic mathematical techniques to some existing figure work, relevant to these matters.*
7. *To record specific conclusions of my own, especially if they appear to break new ground.*

Contents

Appendices

Prologue

Let us begin by travelling back in time, to a distant part of the last century, as the curtain begins to rise on a great naval engagement from the dreadnought era. Packs of grey warships are steaming at full speed on a silver-flecked green sea, trailing dark plumes of funnel smoke. White water, flung up from their thrusting bows, is thrown aside and then falls behind as a churning wake. It is a fine day, but already the long view is limited by mist.

High-flying signal flags flutter and strain against the wind, bringing small patches of bright colour to this scene. As the ships pitch, roll and turn, an occasional glint of weak sun reflects from their bridge windows and scuttles. Battle ensigns, freshly hoisted, stream from every masthead. Silently, almost imperceptibly, turrets train and guns elevate. They are brought to bear on an opposing force, just becoming visible as a vague presence on the horizon.

Within the great ships, charging forward with them, are thousands of unseen men at action stations. Some are in positions of high command, perhaps viewing the scene from a lofty viewpoint. The fortunes of nations could turn on their decisions. Many others are deep below the steel decks, enduring the heat from hungry furnaces or attending to the powerful turbines, alert for any change to the smooth rhythm of machinery. In shell rooms and magazines men work with deadly munitions, making them ready for the gunners to use against an approaching enemy. The occupants must sweat it out, locked down in the danger of these confined spaces, and hope for the best when fighting begins.

Final orders are given to steer an interception course. Lamps flicker: urgent messages are flashed back and forth. Weapons are brought to the ready; ranges and speeds are calculated, then checked and re-checked. Banks of dials and gauges are studied; valves are adjusted; settings are confirmed. It is a time of concentration and preparation, a collective test of nerve and tensing of human faculties. Extreme patience is required, but the minutes seem endless. Somehow they pass, slowly ticking away, counted down one by one, while the range steadily closes.

At last the dreadnoughts speak: their opening salvoes blast across those cold, featureless waters. The tension is broken by this ear-splitting, mind-numbing barrage. What follows rests in large measure on the training of the crews. During the action they can expect to be pushed beyond all normal limits, but discipline and duty must prevail. The imperative is to hit hard, hit often and keep on hitting.

The battle is a kaleidoscope of sound and fury, death and destruction - with blazing guns, flying spray, whirling metal fragments, sudden shocks, falling debris, fumes and fire. Sometimes the enemy is in sight; sometimes not. There are vast explosions: ships full of men are wiped out in moments. Wreckage covers the water and bodies are seen, but there is no time to linger. For a while the range opens, and brings a brief lull to the fighting. Then it all begins again. Hostile shells are arriving from a different direction, and torpedoes have been spotted. The fleet must respond to this challenge: hit hard, hit often and keep on hitting...

Finally, when the day's business is done, as a hazy dusk gives way to darkness, the surviving ships turn away and *head back to a safe anchorage. Many bear the scars of battle on their sides and upper works. Slower now, heavy in the water, disfigured, blackened by smoke and flame, they carry home the weary crews, along with dead and injured. Some ships do not return. The implacable sea has claimed them. Lost beneath it, they too are casualties of war.*

-----oOo-----

1. Battlecruiser Origins

Wanted: Four Admirals

In February 1916, at the height of the First World War, the laying down of four powerful German warships of the Mackensen class became of concern to Britain's Board of Admiralty. Setting aside the possible development of a shallow-draught high-speed battleship, and encouraged by the Commander-in-Chief of the Grand Fleet, they asked the Director of Naval Construction to produce some proposals for the next generation of battlecruisers. His reply was duly considered, and the design option that appeared most suitable received their outline agreement. This was developed over the next few weeks. The results were referred back to the Board, whose full approval was given on 7 April for detailed design to proceed.

New ships of the 'Admiral' class would be the British response to that German initiative. Orders were quickly placed with several firms, including John Brown & Co. They had a solid reputation for building major warships, such as the Queen Elizabeth class battleship Barham and the graceful battlecruiser Tiger. Construction of their particular Admiral began later that year. Four were authorised, intended to follow in the tradition of such famous names as Invincible and Inflexible, Repulse and Renown, Lion and the other 'splendid cats'. However, only one would be completed: HMS Hood. Literally Clyde built, an old term denoting quality, she would prove to be the largest ever British battlecruiser, with a speed of more than 30 knots, 15-inch guns and a belt of main armour 12-inches thick.

2. The Age of Dreadnoughts

Dawn of an Era

A decade previously, battleship HMS Dreadnought had joined the British fleet. Designed in secrecy, and hurried to completion, the Admiralty's aim was to have her in service before any rival nation could get there first. Armed with ten 12-inch guns, protected by armour up to 11-inches thick, and able to steam for long periods at 21 knots, this vessel quickly made all previous battleships obsolete. Her name became associated with an era in naval history, when major powers raced to build (or buy) their own capital ships to dreadnought standards.

The products of heavy industry and modern technology, these sophisticated fighting machines became larger, faster and more powerful. The best were driven by steam turbines, and all had uniform outfits of big guns firing explosive shells. Technical developments allowed battle ranges to grow by many thousands of yards. Opposing forces could engage, while appearing to the naked eye as no more than dark specks making smoke on the horizon.

The Nelson Tradition

One hundred years before that, in the tradition of Admiral Lord Nelson, naval warfare had been quite different. Fighting took place between wooden ships of the line with towering masts and billowing sails. Short-range low-trajectory broadsides were exchanged. Muzzle-loading guns, black powder, grapeshot and cannon balls were 'state of the art'. Men stood by with pistols, swords and grappling irons, ready to swarm onto the decks of their nearest enemy. By 1916, when the battle of Jutland was fought, that variety of close-combat naval warfare still had the power to excite and inspire, albeit from the pages of history books.

The Dreadnought Cruiser

Led by Admiral Sir John Fisher, the Admiralty Committee on Designs devised the ground-breaking HMS Dreadnought. They went on to decide that ships of another new type should be introduced. A major factor was the need to safeguard Britain's sea trade under war conditions. The fastest cruisers armed with the heaviest guns should be available to intercept enemy surface raiders, overwhelm the inferior ships and sweep them from the seas. In broad terms, their other duties could be reconnaissance in force, support for smaller scouting cruisers, rapid concentration to envelope a fleet action, and pursuit of an enemy battlefleet.

Fire power and high speed would take precedence in their design, with physical protection limited to the scale of a belted cruiser - typically, 6-inches of armour. Beginning in 1905, construction programmes were authorised for several dreadnought battleships and the equivalent in fast, big-gunned cruisers. Three of the latter had been built by 1909, and entered service with the Royal Navy, where their weapons, speed, good looks and seaworthiness attracted favourable comment.

HM ships Invincible, Inflexible and Indomitable were the first of this new breed. With a length of 530 feet, a beam of 78.5 feet, displacing 17250 tons and armed with eight 12-inch guns, they were good for at least 25 knots. The generic term 'dreadnought cruiser' or sometimes 'battleship cruiser' was initially applied to them, but the more catchy 'battlecruiser' began to be used by the Admiralty in 1911. With an enthusiastic press and an admiring public, the navy's reputation reached new heights.

3. Battlecruisers in Context

Such 'greyhounds of the sea' were soon absorbed into the body of the Royal Navy. Several classes were built. They became larger and faster, with guns of increasing size. Their protection also began to improve. As design teams strove for the optimum combination of armament, speed and armour, some of the later classes became less distinct from current battleships. This would have drastic consequences for three British battlecruisers, including two of the early ones, during a conflict that was already brewing. The early years of the twentieth century were marked by intense Anglo-German naval rivalry. In the event of war amongst European powers, there was a distinct possibility that opposing battlecruisers would exchange blows.

Fast Wings of the Fleet

From an operational point of view, besides the protection of sea trade, the British reckoned that battlecruisers should be able to serve in several ways as 'fast wings' of the fleet. In a scouting role they could seek out enemy ships and report their whereabouts. (By using superior speed they might then lead an enemy into a trap, where the massed guns of their own side would be waiting.) They could dash forward, using heavy weapons to eliminate lesser opponents, perhaps clearing the way for an engagement between battleships. After a major action they might even finish off damaged enemy stragglers by using guns or torpedoes. However, whatever else they might do, the British 'greyhounds' were not expected to take part in a set-piece engagement with battleships. Those were vessels above their class.

The German Version

German battlecruisers soon followed the first generation of British ships, as a 'must have' in the Kaiser's modern navy. From the outset they were intended to form an independent reconnaissance division of the High Seas Fleet. For this they needed a speed advantage of 3 knots over current battleships. It was also decided that they should have the ability to fight in the front line, if so required. Beginning with SMS Von der Tann, which entered service in 1910, stout armour and good defensive properties were deliberately built into them.

Von der Tann had an advantage of almost 10% in armour and protection (29.8% of total weight) compared with her British contemporary HMS Indefatigable (19.9%). This was mostly achieved by savings in construction of the hull (5.9% lighter) and machinery (3.6% lighter). When they fought each other in the North Sea on 31 May 1916, the German ship rapidly, almost clinically, destroyed her opponent. The four 'splendid cats' did take British battlecruiser design in the German direction, with HMS Tiger (1914) probably the best.

Use with Care

Despite the good looks, large-calibre guns, speed, size and glamorous public image, there remained a limiting factor. Put in the simplest of terms, battlecruisers had lighter armour than battleships built at that time. For their part, the British vessels were not intended or well suited to engage with more powerful opponents. The Kaiser's latest battleships carried more guns and were far better protected. If they were in the offing, the British would rely on superior speed to keep out of harm's way.

In 1913 the next Commander-in-Chief of the fleet (Sir John Jellicoe) stressed the immense value of battle cruisers of the highest speed. He was central to the decision in 1916 to develop the four Admirals rather than build more battleships. His predecessor, Sir George Callaghan, wrote of battlecruisers that their primary function must be that of engaging the battlecruisers of the enemy.

All of this came from men at the top, with no reference to any particular risks involved. Yet, just before the outbreak of war, Jellicoe wrote in a memorandum that it was highly dangerous to consider that British ships as a whole were superior or even equal fighting machines, as compared with those of the High Seas Fleet. Unaware of the finer distinctions between battlecruisers and battleships, the British public had a deep-rooted belief in the quality of their naval forces, including ships of all kinds.

4. Battlecruisers in War

Battlecruiser formations were present in the British and German fleets during the 1914-18 war. Lofty aims aside, they were sometimes used in very pragmatic ways, as when Turkish forts were bombarded by British ships during the Dardanelles campaign, or when German ships made hit-and-run raids on coastal towns such as Scarborough, Whitby and Hartlepool.

When hostilities began, the Grand Fleet was eagerly awaiting its first 'fast battleships'. The five Queen Elizabeth class super-dreadnoughts would carry 15-inch guns and were expected to have a speed advantage of several knots over their predecessors. These highly-regarded ships were limited in number, but there was still a sea war to be fought and won. To that end, up to ten fast battlecruisers were already available and there to be used.

Under the spirited leadership of Vice-Admiral Beatty, in a fleet action or fighting independently, it would be appropriate for the battlecruisers to take on equivalent (or lesser) German ships. They certainly had the weapons and speed to do so. The sufficiency of their armour was another matter, likewise the risky ammunition handling practices they had adopted in order to achieve high rates of fire. Little or no regard seems to have been paid to those factors at the time. Considerations of war have an unruly habit of riding roughshod over negative thinking, due caution and technical niceties.

A South Atlantic Mission
Two of the pioneer battlecruisers, Invincible and Inflexible, were despatched to the South Atlantic late in 1914. They were the principal ships in a force led by Vice-Admiral Sir Doveton Sturdee. It hunted and then

eliminated Admiral Graf von Spee's East Asiatic Squadron. His armoured cruisers, the original Scharnhorst and Gneisenau, had recently trounced the British cruisers Monmouth and Good Hope, sinking them with all hands.

The German ships were confronted at the climactic Battle of the Falkland Islands. After quite a lengthy sea chase, and expenditure of much ammunition by the British, they in turn were sunk. Invincible and Inflexible completed that mission without significant damage or serious casualties. Working within safe limits, they had proved their worth. The nation was delighted.

The Battlecruisers Meet
British battlecruisers were thoroughly put to the test in front-line service, when they fought against equivalent German ships in the North Sea. Opposing formations took centre stage at Dogger Bank (1915) and played a key part at Jutland (1916). All the major vessels returned from the first of these, and only one German armoured cruiser (SMS Blucher) was sunk. HMS Lion, the British flagship, was quite heavily damaged and had to be towed back to Rosyth.

At Jutland the main fleets of Britain and Germany were present, but their engagements were brief. Vice-Admiral Beatty (HMS Lion) led the main contingent of British battlecruisers. Although he enticed the leading German ships within gunnery range of the Grand Fleet, his own were involved in bouts of fierce fighting. On this occasion, a high price was paid. They were out-performed by the battlecruisers commanded by Admiral Franz von Hipper (SMS Lutzow), which endured many hard hits, notably from British battleships.

11

How the Big Ships Performed

Two British battlecruisers were blown up at an early stage, during a running fight with Hipper's scouting group. A third was destroyed in similar fashion, later. Apart from HMS Queen Mary, and the Invincibles when they arrived on the scene, the British fired rapidly but not with great accuracy. All the German ships came through, at first with little or no damage, after demonstrating the effectiveness of their 11 and 12-inch guns.

Tactically speaking, Beatty failed to make best use of numerical advantage and the longer-range heavy weapons of his 'splendid cats'. Poor visibility and signalling problems affected the British process of target acquisition. These factors also delayed the active involvement of four super-dreadnoughts from the Queen Elizabeth class. With a margin of speed over other battleships, they were temporarily attached to his force. Their gunnery proved to be of a higher standard: some telling hits were at last scored on the German battlecruisers.

Admiral Jellicoe (HMS Iron Duke) skilfully deployed his battleships in a long line across the path of the approaching enemy fleet (Admiral Scheer: SMS Freidrich der Grosse). They did solid duty, firing on the broadside with the maximum number of guns. None were lost; most of them emerged unscathed. Twice that day the opposing forces took part in a fleet to fleet naval engagement, and on both occasions the German ships reversed course in the face of concentrated fire. The British line was turned in pursuit, turned again to avoid one attack by enemy torpedo boats, and held back from pursuing the High Seas Fleet in case there should be another.

Battleships Marlborough and Warspite eventually withdrew, respectively damaged by a torpedo strike and by gunfire. With some difficulty, both returned home. All the German dreadnoughts survived these encounters, but several of the lead battleships took heavy hits and the battlecruisers suffered further damage.

The Fighting Ends
The British did have some chances to re-engage with their elusive opponents, but did not take them. This failing was not unique to the big ships. Cruisers and destroyers also allowed units of the enemy fleet to slip through the net. Suspicious movements and events were not followed up. Sighting, as well as fighting, reports were not made at the time. The men were fatigued; mist and smoke made it difficult to identify ships; daylight was running out; communications were spasmodic. Some important intercepts of German radio signals were not passed on to Jellicoe or Beatty after being decoded by experts in 'Room 40' at the Admiralty.

In the North Sea combat zone the Royal Navy suffered from a lack of vision at command level, and there was a general climate that discouraged initiative. This had no place within the suffocating detail of Jellicoe's 75 page 'Grand Fleet Battle Orders'. It was also alien to the formal world of navy hierarchy and protocol in 1916.

The fighting faded away; more and more guns fell silent. Helped by poor visibility, gathering darkness and a fair amount of good luck, Germany's High Seas Fleet - somewhat bruised - crossed over the wake of the British Grand Fleet and finally made its way back to harbour. The Battle of Jutland was over.

A Controversial Outcome
The outcome of Jutland was, and to some extent remains, controversial. No simple answer can be given to the enduring question, "Who won?" For the British, with their long naval tradition and high expectations, things did not go to plan. A great fleet had failed to overwhelm a lesser one. There was a sense of failure, or at least that some valuable opportunities had been missed. Strictly in material terms, Germany felt able to claim a victory. This said, Britain could more easily bear the losses, and the strategic balance of naval power was unchanged.

Something wrong with our ships today...
Three British battlecruisers were lost under the German guns at Jutland, all by way of magazine explosions. Indefatigable, Queen Mary and Invincible – a first generation ship - were destroyed, taking thousands of men with them. The others survived, but several were left battle-scarred. British armoured cruisers also took a beating, with Black Prince, Defence and Warrior either blowing up during the action or sinking later.

During the initial 'run to the south', HMS Indefatigable was hit several times and sank after incurring massive damage, possibly from direct penetration of a magazine (aft) and probably from cordite flash (forward). Then HMS Queen Mary became the major British loss, apparently after being struck in the lightly-protected 4-inch battery. From there, cordite flash - once again - reached the forward magazines, and the ship was destroyed by a series of blasts.

Later that day HMS Invincible took a serious hit on Q turret. The armour there was not thick enough, but she might have avoided being blown apart if the working

14

spaces had not contained stockpiled cordite charges, and if adequate anti-flash precautions had been in force. The British armoured cruisers were confronted by more powerful German ships. As punishment for being in the wrong place at the wrong time, they were shot to pieces.

The German battlecruiser Lutzow eventually had to be sunk by her own side, after sustaining severe hull damage. Of the others, Derfflinger and Seydlitz were the most roughly handled. The latter just managed to struggle home, barely afloat after taking many serious hits. However, both were repaired and put back into service. One pre-dreadnought battleship (Pommern) was torpedoed and sunk with no survivors. The German fleet also lost four cruisers. More than a dozen of the opposing destroyers and torpedo-boats went to the bottom. A breakdown of the human casualties is given in Appendix A.

Reflections on the Fighting
The Royal Navy was disappointed with the outcome, and disconcerted that Jutland had brought such major losses. There had not been a decisive British victory to offset the heavy casualties amongst ships and men. Most of the German fleet had escaped. These reverses were also deeply felt at a national level. A debate began: had Jellicoe over-estimated the threat of German torpedoes and been far too cautious; was Beatty a self-serving glory-hunter, who failed to give maximum support to Jellicoe during the battle? Both men had their supporters and detractors, whose factional arguments took years to subside. It all seemed a poor return for the massive investment in the navy and the bravery shown by those who had fought with the Grand Fleet.

There was more at stake than those two personalities. The British performance at Jutland was blighted by technical failures and problems with systems of command, control and communication. Shells, gunnery, armour, signalling, ship-management, night fighting and tactics: all of these were in need of improvement. The Royal Navy resolved to do better in a return match, but there would not be one. 'Der Tag' (The Day) never came again.

As for the German battlecruisers, it had to be granted that they made up a very capable fighting force. They were fast, well protected, difficult to sink, and their gunnery was disturbingly good. Handled with courage and determination, at one stage they came close to being sacrificed in order to protect other units of the High Seas Fleet. Under fire they proved durable, and none blew up. British battlecruisers performed less well.

5. The Long Shadow of Jutland

Jutland and the Navy

The fighting at Jutland cast a shadow across the British navy. One matter was placed beyond doubt, both by that engagement and the earlier one at Dogger Bank. When battlecruisers fought one another, the German variety proved more than capable of holding their own. Vessels from both sides carried big guns and were certainly not afraid to use them.

It was all very well that British battleships had been able to punish German battlecruisers at Jutland, but what might happen in some future fleet action? If British battlecruisers were drawn into a fight involving heavily armed and better protected German battleships (something previously discounted), there might be losses on an even greater scale. Beyond any doubt, traditional armoured cruisers were too vulnerable to give close support to capital ships when fighting took place.

Events in the North Sea raised matters of acute concern and lasting significance for the British. They began to question the future of battlecruisers, in terms of standing up to fire from heavy guns. More to the point, those in service - or just about to enter it - could hardly be retired in a time of war. What should be done about such large new ships as Repulse and Renown, with 15-inch guns but seriously lacking in armour? Where did it leave the orders recently placed, to build the Admiral class? Measures were urgently needed to strengthen such apparently fragile units of the fleet.

A general lesson was that effective gunnery ranges of 20,000 yards or more were feasible: the maximum range for big ship engagements could not be expected to revert to a rather more convenient 16,000 yards. The implications of long distance plunging fire quickly moved up the agenda. Rather than merely striking the armoured sides of ships, heavy shells could be expected to descend onto their relatively thin decks and turret tops. This factor had to be absorbed into naval thinking, and given higher priority within the principles of warship design. Some twenty five years later, in the arctic waters of the Denmark Strait, a fighting range of 16000 yards would make an unexpected comeback, with dire consequences.

Jutland and the Ship
Design of the John Brown battlecruiser had to be reconsidered. A critical post-Jutland review took place, and some important decisions were made in September – October 1916. The hull armour needed to be thickened, and in particular the main belt should be increased from 8 to 12 inches. Turret and barbette armour also required improvement, along with the internal arrangements for horizontal and other protection. Appropriate instructions were given by the Admiralty to the builder. Further piecemeal changes were made to the ship's defensive capabilities before construction was completed.

It was accepted that these structural additions, partly offset by reductions elsewhere, would make the hull sit deeper in the water, to the detriment of good sea-keeping and perhaps maximum speed. Weight-saving measures included deleting all four rear-facing guns from the secondary armament, two pairs of torpedo tubes and some splinter protection from the funnel uptakes.

6. Birth of a Legend

Vital Statistics

The ship now known as HMS Hood was authorised as one of a class of four, but work on the others was suspended in 1917 and eventually they were cancelled. Naval priorities had changed; post-Jutland doubts continued to beset the battlecruiser as a type of ship. It was quite convenient that most of the Admirals were not far advanced in construction. This lone survivor was launched in 1918 by Lady Hood, widow of the commander of HMS Invincible. The ship was completed in 1920 at the considerable cost of £6.025 million. With no equal in any other navy, the hull had a massive length of 860 feet, a beam of 104 feet and a draught of about 30 feet. The equivalent dimensions of RMS Titanic were 882.75 feet, 92.5 feet and 34.5 feet.

As pioneered by battleships of the Queen Elizabeth class, there were eight 15-inch guns in four twin turrets (A and B forward; X and Y aft). Improved mountings enabled these to elevate to 30 degrees and fire shells weighing 1920 pounds to a maximum distance of 29,000 yards. They were backed up by twelve 5.5-inch guns in single mountings, and four 4-inch anti-aircraft guns. There were six torpedo tubes. Four were mounted in the waist of the ship. Two were submerged, in the hull forward of A turret. Flying-off platforms for small aircraft were positioned on top of B and X turrets.

The Hood was large and well-armed - but also fast, despite exceeding her final legend displacement of 41,200 tons. During full-power trials, when the engines developed more than 150,000 shp, a speed of just over 32 knots was recorded, at a displacement of 42,000 tons. This peaked at 48,300 tons deep load, as later additions were made to the ship. Oil-fuelled, and driven by steam

19

turbines turning four propellers, she was reckoned to have an operational range of 7500 nautical miles at a cruising speed of 14 knots.

Classification of the Ship
Although completed with substantial amounts of additional protection, and emerging much the better for it - more like an esteemed 'fast battleship' - Hood was unable to benefit in full from the lessons of Jutland. Here was a ship with battlecruiser origins, whose 15-inch guns, high speed and a 12-inch belt of main armour qualified her for front-line duty. However, when it came to horizontal protection, given by the thickness of her decks and internal plating, that did not inspire the same confidence. In fairness, and taking a wider view, much the same could be said of earlier dreadnoughts and super-dreadnoughts, some of which remained in service for many years.

The next British battleships, Nelson and Rodney, carried nine 16-inch guns but were not particularly fast. Armour was given priority over speed. Thick protection was concentrated around their vitals. This included 13-14-inches of belt armour and up to 6.75-inches on the protected deck, but regular plating elsewhere. It was described as an 'all or nothing' defensive scheme, based on the most up to date thinking about design principles. In those terms, they were a real improvement on all British capital ships from the dreadnought era, HMS Hood included. Some further battlecruiser designs were considered, but the cut down Admiral class had no successors. Three of the German Mackensens were launched. Not ready in time to see active service, all were dismantled after the end of the 1914-18 war.

To sum up, Hood spent her life as neither a classic battlecruiser nor a fully-fledged battleship. Design changes had complicated and prolonged the construction process. She finally entered service with the high speed of a battlecruiser, as many heavy guns as a contemporary battleship and a scale of protection that fell somewhat short of the mark. It had all been achieved with a substantial and enduring weight penalty.

HMS Hood has been described as a transitional ship. She stood alone, a special ship, the last of her kind built for the Royal Navy. During more than twenty years of faithful service, including many ambassadorial visits, even a high-profile world tour, she acted as flagship of the battlecruiser squadron and was never officially recognised as a battleship.

7. The Mighty Hood
A Ship of Quality

In 1920 'The Mighty Hood' joined the British fleet. The curve and flare of a clipper bow, a graceful length of hull uninterrupted by gun mountings, two large and well-spaced funnels, a balanced massing of the superstructure and a prominent control top marked her out as a beauty amongst warships of the world, a focus of national pride and affection. Until her loss on 24 May 1941, flagship Hood was the largest and most prestigious British warship in service. Her crest read "Ventis Secundis" - With Favourable Winds. It was surmounted by an anchor and a Cornish chough.

The Navy View

The British navy had reservations about this newcomer, extending beyond the adequacy of her physical protection. For example, all the rear-facing 5.5-inch guns had been sacrificed to offset the additional weight of steel that went into her. The bridge arrangements were inefficient, and did not allow all-round visibility. Despite her size it would prove difficult to find space on the superstructure to introduce modifications. It would have been better if some at least of the main magazines had been positioned beneath their respective shell rooms. Specialists within the Admiralty regarded the above-water torpedo tubes as inherently dangerous. Excess weight and restricted freeboard aft were enduring problems, making her a wet ship. At high speeds, there could be severe vibration in the spotting top, whereas a steady perch was needed for the men and the instruments they used.

On the other hand, HMS Hood was one of the fastest ships in service. The main armament could elevate and fire further than any of her predecessors. There were up to date anti-flash precautions between magazines and guns. As against the next generation of British battleships, Nelson and Rodney, her main armament was arranged to give all-round fire. The secondary armament was placed well above the waterline. Anti-torpedo bulges were integral with the hull rather than built onto it. These were provided with metal crushing tubes to help cushion the blast from a torpedo strike. Size helped to make the Hood a steady ship: her slow roll was consistent with being a good gun platform. After making due allowance for length and beam, she was not regarded as difficult to handle.

Structure of the Ship
Some reference should be made to the structural aspects of HMS Hood. Adding more than 4000 tons of armour and protective plating during construction required the hull to be modified and strengthened. Then, as Britain's largest and most prestigious warship, she regularly steamed the waters of the world, 'showing the flag' when and where required. The public did not know that the object of their affection was in an increasingly overweight condition, during more than two decades of service to the nation.

Always known as a wet ship, rough seas would sometimes sweep across the Hood's quarterdeck, giving her the appearance of a half-tide rock. She was even jokingly referred to as the largest submarine in the navy. A small aircraft, catapult and crane were briefly carried, aft of Y turret, but the 'plane suffered damage in heavy weather and those features were removed. The author's modest contribution to the publication 'Sea Classic International' (Summer 1986) emphasised the design-plus stresses and strains of this condition, and questioned

23

whether it could have affected the ship's structural integrity.

A Missed Opportunity
Practical constraints, including the need to modernise older ships, meant that Hood was never taken out of service for a major reconstruction along the lines of those given to the battlecruiser HMS Renown and some battleships of the Queen Elizabeth class. Amongst other changes it was intended to replace the main and auxiliary machinery, reconstruct the bridge and the quarterdeck area and thicken the deck protection. Her old secondary armament would have been replaced. Excess weight such as the torpedo tubes, redundant armour and the substantial conning tower would have been removed.

HMS Hood was called up for duty at the outbreak of war against Germany in 1939, without the benefit of many worthwhile modifications. One significant change was made: the complete replacement of her original secondary armament by an array of dual-purpose four-inch guns.

8. Protection for the Ship

Vertical Armour

The ship's final layout included a substantial main belt of ingeniously angled side-armour, 12-inches thick, for primary protection. There were strakes of thinner armour above, below and beyond this. The main belt extended for more than 500 feet, between the barbettes of A and Y turrets. This gave vertical protection to the 15-inch armament, and a lot more besides. There was a large amount of internal space to be defended, much of it allocated to the boiler and turbine rooms required to propel a high-speed vessel. More information about vertical armour is given in Appendix D.

Horizontal and Plated Protection

When a hostile shell descends at a steep angle, which is quite likely at long battle ranges, it may strike a turret top, a deck, the superstructure, or perhaps an important part of a ship's hull lacking sufficient side armour. If that plunging shell is not to penetrate, and compromise vital installations (magazines, engines, boilers etc) then additional protection is needed on the decks of the ship or within the interior spaces, or both.

As well as vertical armour on the hull, and horizontal defence by way of sturdy decks in high-tensile steel, HMS Hood was provided with other internal measures in the form of armour slopes and protective plating. This was especially important in areas containing the ship's magazines. Appendix D gives more information about those features.

Tests have shown that a given thickness of protection is more effective at stopping the main impact of a shell if it is concentrated in one place rather than being dispersed in several layers. Some of the Hood's protection was multi-layered, spread over various decks, reflecting her battlecruiser origins. It was improved while the ship was being constructed, but there were practical limits to what could be done. By contrast, the main belt armour inspired more confidence. That was provided as a single 12-inch layer, angled to allow a standard of protection somewhat greater than its nominal weight and thickness.

Magazine Protection
The ship's magazines were protected in various ways. The 12-inch belt was of major importance, but other strakes of hull armour, the high-tensile steel decks, armour slopes and internal plating also contributed, as did the reinforced magazine crowns (2 inches thick). According to an article by Paul J Kemp, mentioned below, there was a perimeter of 7000 yards within which the vitals of HMS Hood should have been proof against shells from 15-inch guns. Her dramatic fight with two German raiders, Bismarck and Prinz Eugen, will be examined, later, with that in mind.

9. Internal Arrangements

The following features of the Hood's interior are of particular interest: main magazines X and Y and their shell rooms, all in the rear part of the ship, and a secondary magazine just forward of these.

Main Magazines
The ship had four main magazines, serving the guns of turrets A, B, X and Y. They were situated on the platform deck, shielded by external belt armour, protective decks, crowns and internal plating. Their shell rooms and the secondary magazines were also protected by those measures. Armoured barbettes, extending down into the hull, supported the heavy turrets as well as enclosing ammunition hoists and other machinery.

Magazines X and Y held about 90 tons of cordite charges, stored in brass cases until required for hoisting up and loading into the guns. At that stage they lost their basic protection, and became more vulnerable to fire or explosion. Cordite handling rooms, provided with flash-tight scuttles, separated the main magazines from their turret trunks. The importance of adequate anti-flash arrangements had been shown in stark relief during the fighting at Jutland. Smoke from that battle had scarcely cleared when Vice-Admiral Beatty alerted Admiral Jellicoe to his concerns, rehearsed here at Appendix B.

Fifteen Inch Shell Rooms
These were on the hold deck, below their respective magazines. Armour piercing and high explosive shells were kept in bins - about 120 rounds per gun - until lifted by overhead grabs and loaded into ammunition hoists serving the turrets. Unlike the propellant charges, they were relatively inert and probably safe against hazards other than a severe fire or a direct hit.

The hold deck also provided space for engineering and technical stores, the four boiler rooms, steam turbines and other machinery of many kinds. Below that were the ship's double bottom and main (box) keel. There was crawl space in the double bottom for the cleaning and maintenance of tanks for oil fuel or feed water, but not enough room for a man to stand.

All told, a 100 foot length of the ship was taken up by the magazines, shell rooms, turret trunks, machinery and ammunition handling spaces for X and Y turrets. As part of the post-Jutland thinking, there were proposals to reverse the position of the magazines and shell rooms within ships of the Admiral class so that the more volatile and vulnerable cordite would be stored deeper down, further below the waterline. Applying this to HMS Hood, it seems that the hull lines towards her stern made it quite difficult in the case of Y turret, and other technical considerations generally worked against it. In the event, nothing was changed.

Secondary Magazines
The ship had additional magazines for the subsidiary armament, originally consisting of 5.5-inch surface weapons and 4-inch anti-aircraft guns. Situated adjacent to the 15-inch magazines for B and X turrets, they were also protected as described above. During 1939-40, when HMS Hood was completely re-equipped with an outfit of 4-inch dual-purpose guns, the secondary magazines were converted to store ammunition for the new weapons.

One 4-inch magazine, measuring about 45 feet long by 35 feet wide, is central to an examination of the loss of the ship. This facility extended down to the hold deck from just below the waterline. It sat between X magazine and the aft turbine room, some 25 feet inboard, roughly 300 feet from the bridge and compass platform and 600 feet back from the bow. The significance of these features will become apparent, later. More than 18 tons of ammunition was stored there, to serve what had become the ship's secondary armament.

Magazine Safety
British battlecruisers were severely tested during the Battle of Jutland. Three ships were sunk by way of magazine explosions, and two of them probably had their turret armour pierced. The fate of HMS Invincible was quite clear-cut. A turret roof was blown off. Cordite charges ready for use were ignited. Fire flashed down the trunk enclosing the ammunition hoist, and devastating explosions followed. As recorded at Appendix B, HMS Lion narrowly avoided a similar fate. Prompt action had to be taken to close off and flood a magazine threatened by fire descending from her damaged Q turret.

These events were thoroughly investigated, and some serious lessons learned. Safeguarding measures were recommended for British warships, including flash-tight scuttles between charge-handling (handing) rooms and magazines. The new battlecruiser was duly equipped with these. Also, ready-use charges were not to be stockpiled in turret working spaces: a very dangerous practice adopted for the sake of keeping up a high rate of fire.

10. An Immune Zone
Size, Relevance and Provenance
Imperial War Museum Review No. 4 of 1989 contains an article by Paul J Kemp ('The Loss of HMS Hood, 24 May 1941') which gives some fresh perspectives on a bruising sea battle fought between British and German ships in the Denmark Strait. Amongst other matters, the article proposes that the Hood had a quantifiable 'immune zone'. Her physical protection should have been proof against the heaviest German guns, as mounted on battleship Bismarck, between the ranges 29500 - 22500 yards, equivalent to just under 3.5 sea miles.

The protection given to a major warship by side armour is one dimension of the immune zone. The other dimension is that protection mainly given by horizontal measures, which may be concentrated or layered over several decks. Additional defensive plating between decks is also likely to be found. An immune zone covers the distance from a comparable enemy at which the ship's belt armour cannot be penetrated by hits from low trajectory shells, and the distance at which her lighter plating, protective decks and other internal measures cannot be penetrated by plunging shells fired at longer range. If a warship can engage in a gunnery duel from within an immune zone, that confers a defensive advantage.

Side armour can provide more than its nominal degree of protection if enemy shells strike obliquely. HMS Hood's main belt was angled in the vertical plane, to take advantage of that. Likewise, shells fired from a position ahead or astern of a classic broadside may strike at an angle favourable to the armour protection. With all this in mind, it is instructive to examine the main events of her one and only sea battle.

Relevance to HMS Hood

The concept of an immune zone is important when considering how the ship was handled during the battle of the Denmark Strait. Did her senior commanders know or believe that she had a zone? Was it respected, overlooked in the heat of battle, or perhaps ignored? Arising out of a serious article in a reputable journal, the subject needs to be examined in more detail. As will be seen, it is far from straightforward.

To begin, it cannot be taken for granted that the ship did have an immune zone with the parameters just mentioned. Delineation of a zone became standard practice when new major warships were specified, but this did not happen until well after Hood had entered service. It was first adopted by the USA during the 1930s, and came too late to have been used as an explicit part of Britain's design process for any earlier class of capital ship.

During an official inquiry into the loss of HMS Hood, some information was gathered on immune zones for various British battleships. This implies a lack of data for three battlecruisers in service at the outbreak of the second world war (Repulse and Renown were the other two). Units of the Queen Elizabeth class were listed as the closest to Hood in terms of vertical and horizontal protection. They were apparently best fought at ranges between about 27000-18000 yards, giving a zone of some 4.5 sea miles.

The Five Queen Elizabeths

A brief digression is needed, concerning these pre-Jutland 'super-dreadnoughts'. Their defensive qualities were considered satisfactory at the outset, but it was later accepted that the horizontal protection needed to

31

be enhanced. This was done as part of a rolling programme of improvements, beginning with HMS Barham in 1931. In all probability, their 9000 yard immune zone was not an original calculation, but one carried out years later for the ships as modernised. On that footing, zonal figures from the Queen Elizabeth class were not available as a yardstick against which HMS Hood might have been assessed and ranked as a fighting unit while being designed, or modified during construction, or early on in her career.

In the absence of data for the actual ship, the Queen Elizabeth analogue suggests (but does not prove) that battlecruiser Hood had belt armour providing battleship-quality defence down to something like 18000 yards. Though better than the Kemp figure of 22500, it must be borne in mind that the final part of her engagement in the Denmark Strait was probably fought at a range of 16500 yards. On the other hand, as will be seen, Bismarck was firing from a position ahead of the Hood, so German shells were arriving at an angle favourable to the side armour.

The Zone that Might Have Been
Construction of the ship was a lengthy process, punctuated by fresh thinking on how her standards of protection could best be improved. Although a superior battlecruiser emerged, questions remain as to whether Hood was ever credited with a distinct immune zone. What would have been its limits, when would they have been calculated and who would have known about them? Why were the details not available to the Admiralty inquiry? So many decades later it is not very likely that clear evidence will be unearthed to resolve those matters one way or another. In all the circumstances, references to an immune zone are best

hedged around by cautious terms such as 'apparent' or 'possible'.

The important point is this. Even if some immune zone figures had to be borrowed from a class of battleship, and were only an approximation for the battlecruiser, to be of practical use they did need to be known outside of strict Admiralty circles. It was the kind of information required by Vice-Admiral Lancelot Holland in May 1941, when his flagship went into action against the most powerful unit of the German navy.

11. Background to a Mission
Planning for Operation Rheinübung
During the spring of 1941, as part of Germany's war effort against Britain and her allies, planning began for a group of fighting ships to be sent into the North Atlantic. There they would attack and disrupt long-distance convoys vital for the supply of food, raw materials, oil, weapons and the like. Earmarked for this purpose were the new battleship Bismarck, two battlecruisers and the heavy cruiser Prinz Eugen. On paper, it was a considerable force, but the latter-day Scharnhorst and Gneisenau became unavailable because of machinery problems and damage from an air attack. So, it fell to Bismarck and Prinz Eugen to make this sortie, "Operation Rheinübung" (Rhine Exercise), when they had finished working up to full efficiency in the Baltic Sea.

Battleship Bismarck
Bismarck was a formidable vessel, new to the German fleet and one of the best capital ships afloat at that time. Though not as long as Hood, she was her equal in the number of 15-inch (37.5 cm) guns carried - and better all round for secondary armament as well as anti-aircraft defence. Moreover, Bismarck was of greater tonnage, broader in the beam, better armoured and sub-divided. She could at least match Hood for speed, bearing in mind that the British ship was no longer in her prime. Bismarck also had the advantages of up to date technology, particularly in crucial matters of gunnery control.

Heavy Cruiser Prinz Eugen
Prinz Eugen, another new ship, was a well-balanced design. She carried a main armament of 8-inch (20 cm) guns in four twin turrets, a strong outfit of torpedoes and ancillary weapons, a useful amount of armour, and had

a speed in excess of 30 knots. As in the war of 1914-18, the German navy had ships that could fairly be described as fit for purpose.

Watch on the Rheinübung

When war broke out in 1939, the British Admiralty expected that there would be hostile naval operations aimed at merchant shipping. They were right to do so. German surface raiders were active from an early stage, carrying out such attacks as a deliberate part of military strategy. It was clearly stated in Seekreigsleitung Directive No.1 for the Conduct of the War, 31 August 1939, that the Kriegsmarine would carry out commerce warfare, "aimed primarily against England." Early in 1941 Scharnhorst and Gneisenau returned from a 60-day raiding mission in which they sank 116,000 tons of British shipping (22 vessels). Forewarned being forearmed, the Admiralty needed the earliest possible indication of another sortie of that kind.

There was bad news for the British: Bismarck and Prinz Eugen sailed from Gotenhafen (Gdansk)on 18 May 1941. They were already through the Kattegat, between Denmark and Sweden, by the time that a sighting report from a Swedish cruiser found its way to London. The two ships were next sighted near the mouth of the Skaggerak, passing Kristiansund in German-occupied Norway.

On reaching the North Sea they hugged the coast as far as Grimstadfjord (near Bergen), then paused until the weather closed in and gave cover for their next move. Prinz Eugen refuelled, but her larger companion did not. Aerial photo-reconnaissance confirmed their presence in the fjord on 21 May, and also their absence on 22 May. They had indeed steamed away, taking full advantage of cloud and rain. As a precautionary measure, battlecruiser Hood and battleship Prince of Wales, supported by six destroyers, were ordered to put to sea from the Orkney Islands fleet base of Scapa Flow. They did so, late on the evening of 21 May.

12. Raiders on the Loose

Hide and Seek

This was 1941: air patrols were easily grounded by bad weather; long-distance search radar had yet to be developed; it would be decades before satellite surveillance became possible. Ships could easily disappear into the vastness of seas and oceans. This well suited the German raiders as they headed north into arctic waters. The British dilemma was how to find them and deploy an interception force, before they could break out into the Atlantic and bring havoc to vital sea traffic. Part of the German plan was for Bismarck to deal with any big-gun convoy escorts, leaving the way clear for Prinz Eugen to move in and sink the merchant ships. On the other hand, a naval engagement with superior forces was definitely something they should avoid.

The British knew there were several routes that the German ships could take to reach their Atlantic hunting ground, shielded by the weather and such hours of darkness as were current in those latitudes. However, some were within easy reach of home forces and less likely to be chosen. Until the skies cleared and further aerial reconnaissance became possible, it rested with the navy's thinly-spread surface ships to patrol the raiders' options. As well as HMS Hood and her consorts, the battleship King George V, battlecruiser Repulse and the aircraft carrier Victorious were at sea in a second search force. All were prepared to close in, should a sighting report come through.

Only later did it become clear that the German commander, Vice-Admiral Gunter Lutjens, would be making his way through the Denmark Strait - a remote arctic channel between Iceland and Greenland. The dour and uncommunicative Lutjens was experienced in this respect. On board Gneisenau, in company with Scharnhorst, he had led the previous big-ship operation so fruitful for the German cause. His route towards the Atlantic had included the long and ultimately successful passage around Iceland and through the Strait.

A Sea Hunt
Hood, Prince of Wales and their destroyers were ordered to deploy to the south west of Iceland. That would enable them to cover the enemy's northern routes, namely the Denmark Strait and a passage between Iceland and the Faeroe Islands. County class cruiser HMS Norfolk, already on patrol in the Strait, was about to be reinforced by HMS Suffolk. The latter ship's radar set would play an important role in events to come. The hunting group led by HMS King George V had to cover a potential enemy breakout through more southerly routes, such as the Fair Island Channel (between the Shetlands and the Orkneys) or the wider one between the Shetlands and the Faeroes.

On 23 May, still undetected, Bismarck and Prinz Eugen left open water and entered the icy narrows of the Denmark Strait. Their run towards the Atlantic was going well. The mostly bad weather was helping to conceal them. Rain and mist brought poor visibility; there was also a cold wind and a rising sea.

First Contact
Just before 1930 hrs a keen lookout on HMS Suffolk reported one, then two, ships off to starboard (bearing green 140). The German raiders had been found, at a distance of about 14000 yards. Suffolk made a sharp turn away, to keep clear of Bismarck's guns. From the cover of a fog bank she sent a radio report to inform HMS Norfolk and summon her to the scene. Bismarck and

Prinz Eugen continued on their way. They did not bother to engage the British cruiser, which may well have been detected some time earlier by German radar and hydrophones.

When the two ships had safely passed, Suffolk began to follow. The cruiser tracked them visually as well as by radar. Her set was quite advanced for its day, proving capable over a range of about 12 miles. On arrival of HMS Norfolk, the two cruisers would unite in a shadowing role.

Iced-up radio aerials blocked some of the 'enemy sighted' reports made by HMS Suffolk. The Commander-in-Chief British Home Fleet (Admiral Sir John Tovey, on King George V) had to wait for the vital news. However, HMS Hood did pick up a transmission from the cruiser, and Vice-Admiral Lancelot Holland was ready to act. By 1940 hrs he had ordered the squadron to increase speed to 27 knots and steer an interception course of 295 degrees. The distance to be covered was about 300 miles. Contact with the raiders was expected in the early hours of Saturday 24 May.

A Narrow Escape
At 2030 hrs, as HMS Norfolk emerged from fog, she met the German ships approaching almost head on at a distance of about 10000 yards. Bismarck opened fire. The cruiser escaped direct hits, but shell splinters came on board. A rapid turn away, making smoke, took her back into the comparative safety of local murk. An enemy sighting report, sent two minutes later, did reach Admiral Tovey, whose ships were some 600 miles to the south east.

The British C-in-C now knew the whereabouts of Bismarck and Prinz Eugen, but Vice-Admiral Lutjens knew only of the shadowing cruisers. He was unaware of the British heavy forces already closing in ahead of him. Meanwhile, Vice-Admiral Holland steamed on, carefully maintaining radio silence, and his two big ships hoisted their battle ensigns.

Contact Lost
The two cruisers doggedly followed Bismarck and Prinz Eugen on their transit through the Denmark Strait. As time passed, intermittent snow showers began to affect visibility and the radar plot. Conditions worsened, until all contact was lost just before midnight. It would not be regained for several hours, during which the British forces could only speculate on the whereabouts of their quarry.

Holland reckoned that the German ships, taking advantage of the bad weather, had acted to throw their pursuers off the track. They could have altered course by steering south - or just east of south, the better to avoid the Greenland ice shelf. On that basis, he reduced speed to 25 knots at 0017 hrs on 24 May and followed a more northerly course. Then at 0210 hrs he made another change, now steering towards the east, still hoping for an early morning interception.

Contact Regained - At a Price
It was here that events began to conspire against him. The enemy had not made a tactical course alteration: there had just been a temporary loss of contact. Lutjens was pressing on, regardless of the cruisers in his wake. Being followed by those two vessels was an irritation rather than a major concern. His ships were well ahead of them and making good progress, first towards open

water and then onwards to the wider Atlantic. To cover all eventualities, Holland detached his destroyers to search northwards. Those four ships were never called back, and would later be missed. Two had already departed, in order to refuel. Hood and Prince of Wales continued to follow their own course, which was not helpful to the planned interception.

There was excitement mixed with concern at 0247 hrs, when it was reported that Norfolk and Suffolk had regained contact with Bismarck and Prinz Eugen, proceeding very much as before. On receipt of this important news, Holland quickly ordered his two ships to be turned back onto a more northerly course. Speed was increased to 28 knots. It would take the British just under three hours of hard steaming to recover the situation and make an interception on the best terms they could achieve.

13. Preparations for Battle

Holland Changes His Plan

When preparing for battle on the morning of 24 May, Vice-Admiral Holland was obliged to re-think part of his original plan to intercept the raiders. He had hoped to position Hood and Prince of Wales somewhat ahead of Bismarck and Prinz Eugen. Well-directed gunfire from his ships, approaching from the south east, would threaten the enemy's route towards the open Atlantic. They could fire back from an unfavourable angle, alter course and make a serious fight of it, or even abandon their mission.

Now, following various changes to the speed and direction of the British capital ships, he could not expect to be in such a favourable position. As matters stood, the opposing squadrons were steering almost parallel (slightly converging) courses. An early morning situation report from HMS Suffolk was confirmed when the British sighted two German ships in the far distance at 0535 hrs. Still making 28 knots, Hood and Prince of Wales prepared for immediate action. They also began to operate in close formation. A short arctic night had given way to a bright dawn with improving visibility. The wind was cold, blowing from just north of east.

Bringing On the Action

Faced with an unhelpful 'loss of bearing', and already steaming at maximum speed, the British ships were unable to head off their opponents. Holland decided that a broadside to broadside gunnery duel should take place, but first the range needed to be reduced. The raiders had options. They could decline to fight, and there was now enough room for them to manoeuvre. They might try to outrun their interceptors, or even at that stage double back.

At 0537 hrs, at a range just short of 29000 yards, Hood and Prince of Wales were turned 40 degrees to starboard and adopted a more steeply angled approach to the enemy. As the distance closed, a further 20-degree turn was made. Prinz Eugen and Bismarck, steaming in that order, became a distinct presence off the starboard bow.

Though within gunnery range, and still closing, Holland held fire until about 0552 hrs. Some delay was quite understandable. He wanted to protect the identity of his ships, and give the opposition no incentive to make a quick turn away. He also recognised that the attack had to be decisive. If the raiders were allowed to continue, it would risk a lengthy running battle heading towards the Atlantic. Here it is worth recalling that Bismarck and Prinz Eugen were on a mission to break out and assault the war convoys, while the British ships were there to prevent this.

The British Formation
When Holland turned his ships to starboard they presented a narrower profile to the raiders. That would make their identification more difficult, and provide less of a target if the enemy decided to open fire. Although Hood and Prince of Wales could not bring all their main guns to bear during the initial approach, it would take place at maximum speed and be acceptable within the Admiralty's current fighting instructions.

The two British ships continued to steam in close formation, about 800 yards apart, with a modern battleship - the stronger vessel - still second in line. HMS Prince of Wales was a thoroughly up to date member of the King George V class, superior to the Hood in terms of armour, with more big guns and a better gunnery control system. Rushed into war service, she was untested as an operational unit and unlikely to perform at full efficiency.

Holland kept his battlecruiser in the lead, bearing in mind the Hood's capabilities as a more experienced ship. She was best suited to fight with the thicker side armour exposed, rather than at a range where it would be done with a lesser combination of strong decks and protective plating. Events would soon show that his confidence was misplaced, or at least that his battle plan was flawed in the execution.

14. Battle of the Denmark Strait

The Battle Begins

A short but ferocious gunnery duel began at 0552 hrs, when the British ships opened fire. It quickly became apparent to Vice-Admiral Lutjens that these were not cruisers like Norfolk and Suffolk. The unexpected presence of two heavy ships was a serious challenge to his entire mission. Lutjens had been briefed by naval high command only in extreme circumstances to engage in a sea battle with superior forces, but Bismarck's captain, Ernst Lindemann, was against having his ship simply used for target practice. Big decisions were needed, and they were quickly made. The German raiders returned fire, while continuing to steam ahead. The time was 0554 hrs.

A steep angle of approach meant that the British squadron could only bring their forward turrets to bear. They were also hampered by flying spray from a rising swell hitting the main gunnery rangefinders. At the outset Hood opened fire on Prinz Eugen, mistaking the lead ship for Bismarck. Although their profiles were rather similar, the cruiser was definitely smaller than her companion. When that error was detected, an order was given to rectify it. To her credit, Prince of Wales quickly identified and fired on Bismarck. Hood opened up with the four guns of A and B turrets, while Prince of Wales fired with her six (soon reduced to five) forward guns.

A Question of Range

There is some disagreement about the range when Hood and Prince of Wales opened fire. Some written sources have given it as 25000 yards, or as much as 26500 yards. On the other hand, arising from one of the tables mentioned below, it could have been closer to 21000 yards. By reference to the same table, Bismarck returned fire at a range of about 19700 yards. When the battle began, Hood's course was taking the flagship ever closer to the German ships. Indeed, applying immune zone parameters in the simplest of terms, the range closed so much that even her thickest side armour was vulnerable to 15-inch shells from Bismarck's guns.

HMS Hood Under Fire
Bismarck fired at least five salvoes at the British flagship, using four of her eight heavy guns on each occasion. Beyond that there is limited agreement about the details, even amongst the Hood's survivors. Rather vaguely, the opening salvo has been described as falling ahead of the target, followed by one astern. Another version has the first coming down off the starboard side, while the second was off the port bow. There is no suggestion that either of them fell close enough to have scored any actual hits.

Bismarck's third salvo is usually recorded as a straddle. Number four seems to have been a close short. There is no great certainty about the details of salvo five, which came crashing down at about 0600 hrs. There could have been a single hit on the shelter deck, accompanied by others on the starboard side, above or below the waterline.

The best version of events probably comes jointly from the museum journal article and an account from a survivor. Paul Kemp enumerates five salvoes from Bismarck: some elements can be reconciled with what Signalman Ted Briggs saw and heard. He describes two salvoes in some detail. One was long, while the other involved four shells falling just short of the starboard side of his ship. Bismarck's fifth arrived as Hood and Prince of Wales were starting to make a second turn to port.

Early Hits

When the Germans returned fire, they concentrated on the British flagship. It quickly proved accurate. First blood is credited to Prinz Eugen, whose 8-inch guns scored an early hit on Hood's shelter (boat) deck near to the main mast. A prominent fire was soon blazing there. As well as that hit, another German shell apparently went through Hood's spotting top without exploding. From one survivor's account, dismembered bodies began to fall onto the decks below, and Prinz Eugen might have scored again between the main mast and forward funnel.

According to a German memoir, written nearly 40 years after the event, the first three salvoes fired by Bismarck were, respectively, 'short', 'over' and 'straddling'. The Chief Gunnery Officer then reported "The enemy is burning" and ordered "Full salvoes good rapid". He did not claim the hit which made his target burn. It is likely to have been from a shell fired by Prinz Eugen, when Hood was struck on the shelter deck.

Briggs was present on the Hood's compass platform, and emerged as one of the few survivors. After seeing the distant flash from Bismarck's guns, he heard a salvo pass overhead. Then four high columns of foam, tinted with an erupting dirty brown fringe, appeared not far from the starboard beam. Suddenly he was flung to the deck. The ship had taken a hard knock. Everyone on the compass platform had to scramble back to their feet. A hit on the nearby spotting top could explain why they had just been upended. It was only a prelude to the wholesale carnage that would follow in the next few minutes.

The compass platform was a top tier of Hood's main bridge structure. It provided a high vantage point for an eyewitness, being about 75 feet above sea level and just over 300 feet back from the bow. Ted Briggs had a grandstand view of what was happening, ahead and along the starboard beam (in the general direction of the German ships), but not all round. Much of his own vessel was out of sight, including the whole of the shelter deck and the aft turrets. Only when the Squadron Gunnery Officer ventured outside, and reported back, was it known that a fire had been started by a hit near the base of the main mast.

The blaze on Hood's shelter deck was being fed by exploding anti-aircraft rockets and 4-inch shells, mostly stored in light metal lockers. Although this caused numerous casualties and local damage, an order was given to let it burn out. Briggs was able to hear the screams of injured and dying men coming up through the voice pipes. This setback was not regarded as critical to Hood's main fighting abilities. Though suffering from a flesh wound, she was still a viable fighting ship.

The Loss of HMS Hood - Bismarck's Fatal Salvo
What happened next, at 0600 hrs, is worth recounting in some detail. A blinding flash swept around the outside of the compass platform. Briggs was thrown off his feet for a second time and dumped head-first on the deck. The ship shuddered, then began to list slowly, almost hesitatingly, to starboard for about ten degrees. The helmsman was heard shouting up the voice pipe to the officer of the watch that the steering had failed. The gyro-compass also ceased to function.

Eyewitnesses on other ships recalled how the ominous signs of Hood's internal convulsions were starting to show.

Spouts of flame began to emerge from ventilation shafts leading upward from the turbine rooms, followed by a much greater outburst through her shelter deck between the main mast and second funnel.

This was not evident to those on the compass platform, where order was restored and calm prevailed. Hood was beginning to return to an even keel. Vice-Admiral Holland was soon back in his chair, observing the enemy ships through binoculars. Then everyone present experienced a sudden, horrifying roll to port, which continued until it approached an angle of forty five degrees. According to Ted Briggs, no order was given to abandon ship: indeed, not a word was spoken. They were finished; it was all over; no one needed to be told.

Erupting flame, smoke and steam, the Hood was now a broken ship. Big though she was, the battlecruiser heeled over and sank in a matter of minutes. There is strong evidence from the underwater camera of an expedition to the Denmark Strait that the searing blast was powerful enough to have shattered a significant length of the ship's hull and opened up the interior. It could even have penetrated as far as the forward magazines, adding to the general devastation. An account of these events, as seen from Prinz Eugen, appears at Appendix E.

High Drama
The author Ernle Bradford depicted the climax of the battle in this dramatic way: "At a range of 16,500 yards the Hood had received her death blow. A pillar of fire soared into the air - a thousand feet high. Guns and turrets were plucked from their mountings and tossed aside like toys. Masts collapsed, hundreds of tons of steel rained on to the water, and the northern sky was split by

thunder. She heeled to port. Her back broke. Her bows and stern lifted like two great tombstones to her dead."

In less than five minutes from the arrival of Bismarck's fatal salvo HMS Hood had been destroyed, along with very nearly her whole crew. Ted Briggs was one of just three survivors out of more than fourteen hundred men. Two of those on the compass platform narrowly escaped as the stricken ship went down. There was one other survivor, who had been present on the shelter deck.

Prince of Wales Continues the Fight
From that point on, battleship Prince of Wales was left alone to continue the fight. She did manage to score a few hits on Bismarck, inflicting some important damage. One shell penetrated the hull and deprived the German ship of part of her fuel supply, which resulted in the raiders' mission being curtailed. Soon, though, the British ship began to pay the price for having made her approach in close formation with Hood.

The German ships found it easy to switch targets, following the demise of the British flagship. Before long, mauled by the concentrated gunfire of her opponents, and unable to make adequate reply, Prince of Wales ended the engagement and moved to a safe distance under cover of smoke. Bismarck, slightly down by the head and leaking fuel oil, had to withdraw from Operation Rheinübung. Later she provided covering fire when Prinz Eugen was given permission to break away and continue on into the Atlantic.

15. Inquest

The Loss of HMS Hood - Admiralty Boards of Inquiry

The Admiralty convened two official Boards of Inquiry into the loss of HMS Hood, which for many years had been a national favourite, the largest and most prestigious of warships. Sir Dudley Pound, First Sea Lord, commented that it was "disturbing" and a "disaster", which seemed to bear remarkable similarities to the loss of three battlecruisers at Jutland. The first Board (under Vice-Admiral Sir Geoffrey Blake) reported on 2 June 1941, and the second Board (under Rear-Admiral Harold Walker) on 12 September.

Although the outcome of Inquiry No. 1 was regarded as unsatisfactory, it did record that a hit or hits from Bismarck's fifth salvo blew up the British ship. One may have been near to the mainmast, but the actual position was not corroborated. The result was a large explosion, which appeared to be at the base of the mast. The magnitude of the explosion and the rapidity with which the ship sank indicated that one or more of the after magazines had exploded, causing a large area of the outer bottom plating to be blown out.

So far so good, but the Inquiry admitted that what was witnessed was difficult to associate with the explosion of the 4-inch magazine. Its forward bulkhead was located more than 60 feet aft of the mainmast. Was there an alternative explanation? Although a 15-inch shell fired from Bismarck at the range and inclination of the fatal fifth salvo, and possessing sufficient fuse delay, could have reached the aft magazines, the Director of Naval Construction argued that it was equally likely to have been an explosion in one of the Hood's upper deck torpedo compartments, carrying enough force to break the back of the ship and cause her to sink.

51

Dissatisfaction with that set of proceedings prompted the Admiralty to convene Board of Inquiry No. 2. This was very thorough in the way it called eyewitnesses and took expert opinion. It produced a more robust report which similarly found that "The sinking of the Hood was due to a hit from Bismarck's 15-inch shell in, or adjacent to, the 4" or 15" magazines, causing them all to explode and wreck the after part of the ship. The probability is that the 4" magazines exploded first". This inquiry rejected a line of argument that the ship was lost because battle damage had led to a torpedo compartment explosion.

A Spirited Defence
A former Admiral of the Fleet, Lord Ernle Chatfield, reacted to some press speculation about a possible miscalculation during the design of the ship. He mounted a spirited defence in a forthright letter to The Times of 28 May 1941, pointing out the 22 year age difference between Hood and Bismarck. During that time, engineering science and the power-weight ratio for warships had very significantly changed. In his view, Hood was the most powerful ship of her speed that could have been constructed in her day. If a heavy shell happened to penetrate the armour of a warship at the angle of descent given by long ranges, the chance of one of the several magazines being ignited was quite considerable.

He went on to emphasise how, after the 1914-18 war, and much experiment, it was concluded that a very fast ship could not afford to sacrifice armour to get high speed. So, in the Nelson class of battleships, speed was sacrificed to ensure protection against sudden annihilation by shell, torpedo or bomb. Since Nelson and Rodney were built, modern engineering had closed the gap between those two factors. The Hood was destroyed because she had to fight a ship 22 years more modern than herself. He concluded that her loss was the direct responsibility of those who opposed the rebuilding of the British Battle Fleet until 1937 - and it was only fair to her gallant crew that this should be recorded.

An Eternal Triangle
There is much to commend in his letter. For a given type of warship, designers are faced with a three-cornered trade-off between weapons, speed (size and weight of machinery) and protection. More of one thing usually means less of another. More of everything means a ship of greater size and displacement, longer construction time and greater expense. When the navy acquired a battlecruiser, the emphasis was on weapons and speed. A battleship was slower, but at least as well armed and better armoured. Those design options illustrate a trade-off between speed and protection.

Technological change has provided a way forward from this dilemma. If the size and weight of machinery can be reduced, without sacrificing speed, the savings are available for better protection, more powerful weapons, or both. If new kinds of steel, or new thinking about how it is used, can lessen the weight of armour, without detriment to protection, that saving is available for weapons or speed, and so on. This theme was central to Chatfield's letter. He rightly stressed how an older ship like Hood had been outclassed by a newer one like Bismarck: it was all down to progress in the design and construction of warships.

No More Battlecruisers
With his background, Chatfield knew that battlecruisers were no longer being built for the British navy, and it had been the case for many years. Still powerful but not fast

enough, Nelson and Rodney had been superseded by the King George V class of 28 knot battleships. They were well-balanced vessels, with weapons, speed and protection more suitable for current front-line duty. Compared with these, the once "Mighty Hood" was old technology.

The Official Verdict
There was much public and private grief over the loss of this famous British ship and most of her crew. It was a blow to national morale, at a time when the war against Hitler's Germany was into a second year and not going very well. The circumstances were duly investigated, with much earnest thought applied to the subject. Now there had to be an official verdict, and it drew a line under the Admiralty Boards of Inquiry.

Everything considered, no blame was attached to Vice-Admiral Holland for his tactics, or to the commander of HMS Hood (Captain Ralph Kerr) or indeed to anyone involved with her deployment in that fatal meeting with the German raiders. The First Sea Lord signed a final memorandum to that effect. It was accepted that the tragedy just had to be numbered amongst the misfortunes of war. Nevertheless, with the passage of time, how the British ships had been handled came to be reviewed in a more critical light.

This work gives most attention to the following: failure to concentrate British forces on the morning of the battle; details of the deployment of Hood and Prince of Wales, including the failure to make use of their main armament at an earlier stage, and the extent to which the range was allowed to close while they were approaching Bismarck and Prinz Eugen.

16. Crunching the Numbers
Deployment of HMS Hood - Course, Speed, and an Immune Zone

A table of figures was required, to further explore the details of this sea battle and the implications of a specific 'immune zone' for HMS Hood. It would need to correlate the events, their timing, the changing distance between the two squadrons, and the ship's deployment relative to an immune zone.

The more sources examined while researching these matters, the less there proved to be a consensus on all of the key features. The times of events lined up well enough, but the important gunnery ranges were much less certain. Contradictions were found within and between sources. A few of the values given were so unlikely that they had to be discarded. Uncertainties about the size and status of an immune zone have already been mentioned.

Time and Distance

Fortunately, sources were rather more consistent over the opening and closing events for the required table. On this footing, the two German ships were sighted at 0535 hrs and a distance of 29920 yards (17 miles). That was beyond the outer limit of Hood's immune zone, according to the Kemp article and the Queen Elizabeth analogue. A radio report of the sighting went from Prince of Wales to the Admiralty at 0537 hrs.

Likewise, there was a good measure of agreement that the British flagship blew up at 0600 hrs (and had sunk by about 0603), at a distance of 16500 yards from the guns of Bismarck. These events provided a time-frame of some 25 minutes and a range that closed by about 13420 yards. From those figures, on a simple calculation, the range decreased at a mean rate of 537 yards per minute.

17. What a Table Can Show - No. 1

A Simple Plot

This table plotted a constant rate of change, in effect a straight line, between the upper and the lower ranges: 29920 yards, reducing to 16500 yards. Then, within a framework of 25 minutes, the intermediate values for specific events could be located and the ranges compared with those given in the sources examined.

The table was also sub-divided to reflect various course changes and angles of approach adopted by the British ships. The results were as follows -

Phase 1. 0535 - 0537 hrs (2 mins). Opens with visual contact made; opposing ships are slightly converging; closes when the British turn 40 degrees to starboard (now steering course 280). The range decreases from 29920 yds. to 28846 yds.

Phase 2. 0537 - 0549 hrs (12 mins). Opens with Hood leading the angled approach; closes when the British make a further turn of 20 degrees to starboard. The range decreases to 22405 yds.

Phase 3. 0549 - 0557 hrs (8 mins). Includes the opening salvoes from both sides. Blaze begins on Hood's shelter deck. Closes with a British turn of 20 degrees to port (back to course 280). The range decreases to 18110 yds.

Phase 4. 0557 - 0600 hrs (3 mins). Hood blows up and begins to sink during a further turn of 20 degrees to port. Final gunnery range: 16500 yds.

The next steps involved examining those 25 minutes, to identify the whereabouts of HMS Hood relative to an immune zone extending either between 29500 and

22500 yards or between 27000 and 18000 yards. These details emerged -

0536 hrs: Range down to 29383 yds. Hood has entered a Kemp zone.
0541 hrs: Range down to 26699 yds. Hood has entered a Queen Elizabeth zone.
0549 hrs: Range down to 22405 yds. Hood has left a Kemp zone (inner limit of 22500 yards), before opening fire.
0552 hrs: Range down to 20794 yds. Hood opens fire.
0558 hrs: Range down to 17574 yds. Hood has left a Queen Elizabeth zone (inner limit of 18000 yards), after opening fire.

According to the museum journal article, when Hood opened fire at 0552 hrs the range was 25000 yards: inside the edge of the immune zone. However, this table gave an earlier time for a range of 25000 yards: 0544 hrs. It also gave a closer range at the time of opening fire: 20794 yards. When Bismarck returned fire at 0554 hrs, the table gave the range as 19721 yards.

The Big Question
Working with the opening and closing events, plus the table's intermediate ranges, there was an important question to be answered. When did HMS Hood steam closer to the Bismarck than 22500 yards or 18000 yards - the possible inner limits of an immune zone, as described above?

According to this table, and on the least favourable figure, it had happened by 0549 hrs. The zone had been breached before the British ships opened fire. On the more generous figure, it had happened by 0558 hrs:

both sides were firing and Hood had received her first hits.

Not in the Zone
There was no doubt over the most significant point arising from this. The table showed that HMS Hood may have begun, and clearly ended, her eight minute engagement at less than an apparently 'safe' distance. Most sources gave figures confirming that the final gunnery range was beyond even the best case (Queen Elizabeth) immune zone.

HMS Hood (and HMS Glorious) The Late-War Battlecruisers, c. 1917-1920

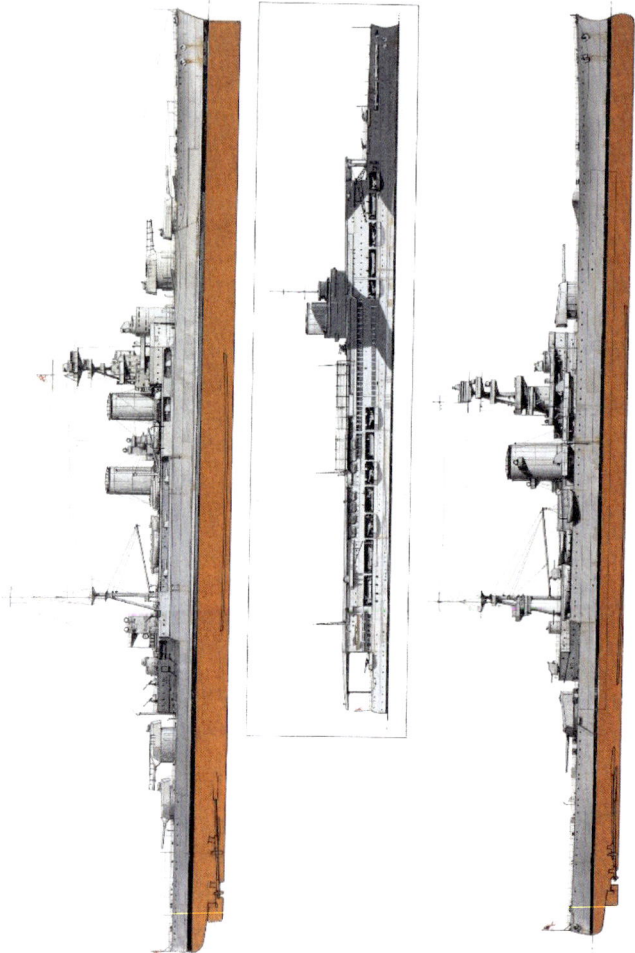

HMS Hood Engaging the Bismarck 24 May 1941

HMS Hood, 1941

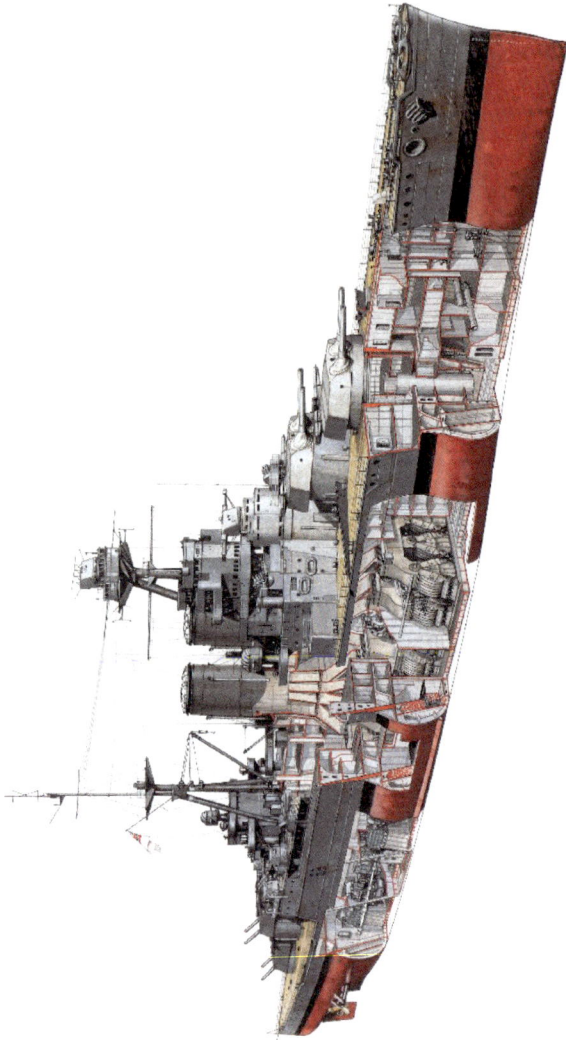

18. What a Table Can Show - No. 2

Filling a Hole in the Table

The table was helpful, but something of major interest lurked unresolved in the data assembled for it. What if the museum journal article was correct in stating that the British ships opened fire at a range of 25000 yards and a time of 0552 hrs? How would it affect other matters, such as fighting from within an immune zone and a final range of 16500 yards at 0600 hrs?

When the table was prepared, ranges were treated with much caution. Overall, the time scale was given precedence because it seemed more reliable than many of the ranges quoted for specific events. Perhaps the deployment of HMS Hood would deserve to be assessed rather differently if those two factors, time and range, were given equal weight at one interim point. This alternative scenario was worth serious consideration. Another table was called for.

Scope of the Second Table

Taking on board a Kemp combination of time and range, the second table was prepared along these lines. After the first enemy sighting at 0535 hrs and a range of 29920 yards, HMS Hood steamed for 17 minutes (opening salvo at 0552 hrs) and covered 4920 yards (range 25000 yards).

This also gave a simple straight line plot, for a closing rate of just under 290 yards per minute. Allowing the ship to continue in that way for a further 8 minutes, until 0600 hrs, added 2315 yards to the distance covered. The total became 7235 yards, quite close to the size of a Kemp immune zone, and the final range was a healthier 22685 yards.

Table No. 2

The second table showed the following -

Phase 1. 0535 - 0537 hrs (2 mins). Opens with visual contact made; opposing ships are slightly converging; closes when the British turn 40 degrees to starboard (now steering course 280). The range decreases from 29920 yds. to 29341 yds.

Phase 2. 0537 - 0549 hrs (12 mins). Opens with Hood leading the angled approach; closes when the British make a further turn of 20 degrees to starboard. The range decreases to 25868 yds.

Phase 3. 0549 - 0557 hrs (8 mins). Includes the opening salvoes from both sides. Blaze begins on Hood's shelter deck. Closes with a British turn of 20 degrees to port (back to course 280). The range decreases to 23553 yds.

Phase 4. 0557 - 0600 hrs (3 mins). Hood blows up and begins to sink during a further turn of 20 degrees to port. Final gunnery range: 22685 yds.

Results from Table No. 2

Amongst other matters, the table produced these details -

0537 hrs: Range down to 29341 yds. Hood has entered a Kemp zone.
0546 hrs: Range down to 26737 yds. Hood has entered a Queen Elizabeth zone.
0552 hrs: Hood opens fire, at a range of 25000 yards.
0600 hrs: Range down to 22685 yds. Hood blows up and begins to sink, without having left either of these immune zones.

Table 2 gave the range as 24421 yards, when Bismarck returned fire at 0554 hrs.

Still in the Zone
Working with this alternative table, for various time and range combinations, the same important question needed to be answered. When did HMS Hood steam closer to the Bismarck than 22500 yards or 18000 yards, the possible inner limits of her immune zone? Table 2 showed that she had not done so by 0600 hrs. Contrary to the first set of findings, HMS Hood's battle took place entirely within an immune zone, whether according to Kemp or the battleship analogue.

Mixed Messages
Taken together, the museum journal figures of 0552 hrs and 25000 yards are inherently more generous to Vice-Admiral Holland. The second table, based on them, does show his conduct of the battle in a more positive light, as to the range at which the British ships fought. On the other hand, as explained in Appendix G, those figures are not compatible with the generally given distance of 16500 yards at which Bismarck's fatal salvo struck home.

This difficulty is left unresolved by the article, which does cite 16500 yards as the final range. It is worth mentioning that the tables also differ over the average speed at which the British ships closed with their German opponents. Table 1 gives 537 yards per minute (nearly 16 knots). This is much faster than table 2, which shows 290 yards per minute (just over 8 knots).

Bearing in mind how Holland carried out his ship deployment, why it was done in that way, and recognising some weaknesses apparent in the second table, the odds are that the gunnery range was more like 16500 than 22685 yards, and the closing speed was comfortably above 8 knots.

Methodology and Accuracy
A note about the methodology for these tables appears at Appendix G. When it comes to passing judgement on which is the 'right' set of figures, it is clear that the tables are in competition. They make selective use of the information available, and give different results – although table 1 has rather more credibility. Without advancing any extravagant claims to accuracy, they do at least represent a serious attempt to set out events in chronological order and make better sense of the various ranges put forward as applicable during this battle. They also highlight how an otherwise reliable article can contain an undetected anomaly.

Into Dangerous Waters
Nothing arising from any of these calculations would have prevented the British ships from opening fire with all their fourteen and fifteen-inch guns at an earlier stage and longer distance. As time elapsed, the gunnery range decreased towards 16500 yards. Vice-Admiral Holland continued to close with the enemy, even while adjusting his course to port, and ventured into what proved to be very dangerous waters.

Did Holland get the deployment of his flagship right or wrong in terms of an immune zone of either size considered? The verdict there is less than clear-cut, but the balance of probability goes against him. In any event it does not change the 20 minute duration of his steep-angled approach to the raiders or the timing of his final turns to port. HMS Hood was being hit by one German ship, and straddled by the other, while the first turn was taking place. That was self-evident, and did not depend on anyone knowing about immune zones. She was destroyed before the second turn could be completed.

19. Four Main Theories
The Loss of HMS Hood
There are several theories to account for the loss of the ship. Four main ones will be examined, and two are consistent with the Admiralty findings -

a. Explosion of an above-water torpedo compartment.
b. A 'misfire' within X turret.
c. Magazine explosion (4-inch ammunition).
d. Magazine detonation (cordite charges for X and Y turrets).

Theories Examined
What follows is based on careful study of various published sources, some of which include details from eyewitness accounts, along with plans and sections of the ship. Through it all, a rapidly expanding internal fire of great ferocity must be explained. Quite unlike the bursting of any combination of German shells, it had the appearance of a volcanic eruption taking place on board.

a. Explosion of an Above-water Torpedo Compartment.
Was there a detonation of above-water torpedo warheads and perhaps the torpedo launching charges, either as a result of Prinz Eugen's initial hit, or following the arrival of one of Bismarck's salvoes? Could it have destroyed main strength girders in the waist of the ship, leading to a massive structural failure and her rapid sinking? One Admiralty expert, the Director of Naval Construction, clearly believed that could be the case, although his view was not supported when Board of Inquiry No. 2 submitted its report.

No vast quantity of explosive materials was required to service the ship's above-water torpedo tubes. It amounted to a couple of tons of warheads and firing charges, dispersed in two groups (port and starboard) on the upper deck adjacent to the main mast. Torpedoes in the tubes were protected by external doors, as thick as the hull in that area, and by armoured mantlets - box structures - inside the ship.

Admiralty Boards of Inquiry
The DNC argued that a shell could have detonated the torpedo warheads in one of the pairs of above-water tubes, seriously damaging a part of the ship already affected by impact and fire from the initial hit. Taken together, a structural failure in the upper part of the hull and the effect of water entering the damaged side may have been enough to break the back of the unfortunate Hood.

Here it should be mentioned that the British believed the first hit had been made by Bismarck, not Prinz Eugen. The DNC's position assumed a cumulative effect of heavy shells striking from successive salvoes, penetrating and inflicting real structural damage. Only in the fullness of time was the record corrected in favour of the German cruiser, which had scored at least one hit on the shelter deck. Although a prominent fire broke out, and there were numerous casualties, the big ship shrugged off this light shell.

Board of Inquiry No. 2 concluded that the detonation of torpedo warheads was possible, but there was no direct evidence that it had actually taken place. A sharp explosion of that kind had not been witnessed, and in any case, it could not have accounted for the huge column of flame observed at the time. Their verdict was that Hood's torpedo warheads may or may not have exploded, but this could not have caused the loss of the ship. Nor did they consider that the blaze on the shelter deck contributed to it.

Case Unproven
Even if it had happened, and been of local importance, an explosion in an above-water torpedo compartment on the upper deck could hardly have despatched so large a vessel so quickly and with so much damage. It also lacked a clear and rapid route to the magazines further aft and deeper down in the ship - a distance of about 70 feet. Whether or not they were intact at the time, Hood's torpedo compartments were completely destroyed by a searing blast which rose up from below and devastated a large part of the ship. There is more about this subject in Appendix H.

b. A 'Misfire' within X Turret.
This sequence of events could just conceivably explain the destruction of HMS Hood. It all began with a gun problem in X turret. The gun had to be loaded, with a shell weighing 1920 pounds and a further 428 pounds of cordite propellant. While that was taking place, or when the gun was fired, there was a powerful explosion at the breech end. The interior of X turret was devastated by this blast, and it was of sufficient force to overwhelm the anti-flash measures protecting the magazine below.

When the turret explosion entered X magazine, via the handing room, some propellant charges, ready for hoisting up to the guns, were ignited. There was sympathetic ignition of the remaining magazine contents (more than 40 tons of cordite). A chain reaction followed, involving the ignition of adjacent magazines. With a large part of the ship's hull torn apart by this, her sinking took place in short order. For reasons of brevity here, the misfire theory and a remark giving rise to it are examined in more detail at Appendix I.

A Misfire Considered

Although it has dramatic appeal, that chain of events suffers from some important drawbacks. According to eyewitness accounts from other ships, the first signs of Hood's internal distress were seen on her shelter deck between the main mast and second funnel. A raging fire was beginning to escape through turbine room ventilation shafts.

Inconveniently for the misfire theory, X turret was about 140 feet aft of the main mast. This turret, and the adjacent hull, were not immediately affected by a magazine incident of that kind. Though 65 feet back from the mast, the 4-inch facility was at least situated adjacent to a turbine room. It was a more likely origin for the first outpouring of flame.

The German account at Appendix E is supportive of this. Although one of the aft turrets was blasted clear of the ship, the events described did not begin with a massive detonation in X or Y magazine. Disaster worked its way towards the stern, having started further forward, and not vice-versa.

Another consideration is that X turret was unable to bear on the enemy until late in the battle, because of the narrow angle of approach adopted by the British ships. It is not clear whether that turret fired more than once. The explosion of a defective weapon cannot be ruled out, but there is no evidence to shed light on this. The same can be said about an accident arising from some kind of obstruction in a gun barrel.

Even allowing for the tense circumstances of guns being loaded or reloaded under battle conditions, it would be very surprising if there had been a fundamental failure of system safeguards, or of basic turret drill, on an experienced ship. Also, in this case, the specific post-Jutland anti-flash precautions would have had to be defeated.

c. Explosion of Four Inch Magazine.
This event concerns the aft part of the ship, probably at the beginning of a series of internal blasts resulting from a direct hit by Bismarck. Detonation of the whole or most of 18 tons of ammunition would have caused severe local damage and been visible on the shelter deck. Originating so near to large internal spaces, the turbine rooms, it could have broken the ship's back or opened enough of the hull for flooding to have done so. That alone might have been sufficient to sink her.

The above is consistent with the second Admiralty Board of Inquiry into the loss of HMS Hood. According to their report, "the probability is that the 4-inch magazines exploded first". Destruction of this area would have taken place adjacent to the main magazines for X and Y turrets.

d. Detonation of Cordite Charges (X and Y magazines).
The most likely scenario for this is a sequence touched off by the 4-inch magazine. A huge cordite fire in the main magazines would be quite compatible with an outpouring of flame which spread from the shelter deck area and enveloped a large part of the ship, in line with eyewitness testimony. Those magazines were low down in the hull. Such an event would have destroyed enough of that structure for the ship's back to break. It would

readily explain her loss, and also be consistent with the second Admiralty Board of Inquiry.

Stored deep below the waterline, shells for the 15-inch guns of X and Y turrets should have been relatively impervious to most hazards. Some may have detonated during the fire in X and Y magazines one deck above, adding their own explosive payload, but most of them probably parted company with the ship when a large section of the bottom was blown out.

20. Hunt the Salvo

Eyewitness accounts, the proceedings of two Boards of Inquiry, and more recent underwater exploration of wreckage in the Denmark Strait, all point in the same direction. Nothing short of the detonation of one or more magazines can account for the massive damage to, and rapid sinking of, such a large armoured warship.

This examination of those events would be incomplete without a close look at two related matters which continue to be debated. If the root cause was a hit or hits from battleship Bismarck, is it quite clear which salvo was responsible? Furthermore, exactly where was the ship struck? They are considered here, and under Section 24 (Completing the Picture - The Main Possibilities). Appendices E - F also go into them.

The account from on board Prinz Eugen (at Appendix E) is a useful starting point. This helps to fill some gaps left by the British version of events. Apparently, "a whole salvo" of 15-inch shells from the German flagship reached its target. There is a graphic description of how a violent explosion took place between Hood's second funnel and mainmast, but it does not say whether the initial impact was on her shelter deck or the hull, or both. Could any shells have struck below the waterline? There is no mention of splashes along her starboard side. Also, it fails to place the salvo amongst those fired by Bismarck after 0554 hrs: there are five to be pinned down.

This account boldly claims four German hits, and fails to answer some major questions. Nevertheless, several useful inferences can be drawn from it. Nothing there can be confused with Bismarck's salvoes one and two, which are distinct in having fallen clear of the British flagship with no discernible effect. Nor does it bear any relation to number three, which is typically recorded as a straddle (no definite hits).

Bismarck's fourth salvo fell just off the starboard side of the British ship. A blaze flared up on Hood's shelter deck after it was hit by one of Prinz Eugen's shells at 0557 hrs. There was also some damage to the spotting top. Could there have been an underwater strike, and did fire in the magazines begin at that stage? Other information is available, and some calculations are possible, to shed more light on this - as shown at Appendix F. The German account requires Hood to blow up as a salvo strikes, but that had yet to happen. Until it did, she steamed on.

This 'close short' from Bismarck is not the strongest candidate for having brought about the destruction of flagship Hood. Place, time and other events work against it. When these factors are examined, they help to build up a picture of the dramatic last few minutes in the life of a doomed ship. Accordingly, it is her fifth that comes across as main contender for the title of 'killer salvo'.

After eliminating the less likely salvoes (one short, one long, one straddle and one close short), this work continues to focus on Bismarck's fifth. Despite its major importance, that salvo remains something of an enigma for lack of hard information. One shell may have struck Hood on the shelter deck. It is not clear what became of the others. A few British eyewitnesses referred to splashes alongside, but there is no consistency or consensus over that. No precise impact point, or points, may ever be established.

21. Prelude to Disaster
Deploying the Flagship
One significant point arises from the possibility of an immune zone, whether extending down to 22500 or to 18000 yards. Vice-Admiral Holland may have closed the range to such an extent that his flagship's side armour was no longer safe against hits from Bismarck. As a gunnery expert, he would have been familiar with how a warship could be vulnerable to enemy shells striking with a steep or a shallow trajectory.

He needed to attack from where potentially fatal hits from Bismarck should have been defeated by Hood's high-tensile steel decks and her protective plating or, preferably, by the available belt armour. Either way, the hull would have been less easy to pierce, at an angle allowing any shell to reach a magazine. It is clear that something went very badly wrong. Perhaps it was down to an error of judgement, or even a lack of caution. At a fundamental level, did those in command of the ship have a sufficient grasp of her ability to take punishment?

Holland knew that his ships had arrived late and were out of position: the enemy were in sight, but he could not head them off. A lengthy engagement might be required, with both squadrons heading towards the Atlantic. One option was to close the range and try to force an outcome without a long gunnery duel, although that could hardly be guaranteed. For his flagship and those on board, it lasted just eight minutes.

Using the Guns
When the British ships began their attack, only ten main weapons were able to bear on the enemy. Things did not go well for the flagship, from an early stage. Disadvantaged by the original confusion between Prinz

76

Eugen and Bismarck, Hood really needed - but was not given - a breathing space in which to find the right target. Having identified the two approaching ships as serious opposition, the Germans made a bold decision to fight rather than fly.

Although the battlecruiser's A and B turrets delivered six or more salvoes in the course of a short engagement, there is no evidence that either of the raiders was threatened by any of them. Despite a lack of experience and various technical problems, battleship Prince of Wales managed more than a dozen salvoes. Not all of her main guns fired throughout, and one turret jammed when the ship made a turn, but some hits were scored on Bismarck.

Had she been allowed to fight at longer range and on a more favourable bearing, the flagship would most likely have delivered a better performance. As it was, she achieved nothing and was destroyed in the process. Likewise, Prince of Wales did not need to be positioned quite so close at hand, with little freedom to manoeuvre and use the 14-inch weapons in her three turrets.

The British ships could have steamed in open order, made a tactical turn to port after closing the range to about 23000 yards, and then opened fire. At the risk of being identified a little sooner, and having the German ships take prompt evasive action, a maximum number of weapons would have been available there and then.

In proceeding as he did, Vice-Admiral Holland did not make life easy for his gunnery controllers. The enemy were granted some valuable decision-making time, and his turns to starboard also enabled them to pull ahead.

As battle was joined, that morning interception showed signs of developing into an unwelcome sea chase.

What if a broadside battle had begun at an earlier stage, along those lines, with the British ships not making their second turn to starboard? The opposing forces could have engaged closer to beam on, with Hood kept at a range safely within either of the immune zones considered, and on a course where all four turrets would bear. Similar considerations apply to battleship Prince of Wales. One of her forward guns was destined to fail almost immediately, but the aft turret would have been able to join in the action.

It seems a missed opportunity that Bismarck was not challenged sooner, by a greater concentration of British firepower, while those in command of her were undecided over what to do. If Holland had deployed his forces in that way, and directed accurate fire against Bismarck with all the heavy weapons at his disposal, important early hits might have been scored. As against Bismarck's eight, the British ships had a combined total of eighteen guns. They could have been better used.

22. Decisions, Decisions

For and Against the Vice-Admiral

The following can always be argued on behalf of Vice-Admiral Holland. First, he had clearly surprised the enemy. Lutjens was not expecting heavy units of the British navy to be approaching: suddenly he was on the back foot. Although Bismarck and Prinz Eugen might manoeuvre and try to get away at high speed, where would that leave his mission? Should he turn back or press on? German High Command would not be pleased if two precious ships from the Kriegsmarine became involved in a sea battle, and were damaged - or worse - while he continued with it.

Holland calculated that closing the range would be advantageous to his interception and increase the chances of scoring early hits, possibly decisive to the outcome. During a lengthy battle of broadsides, the German ships might be able to edge away and escape towards the Atlantic. That would be a bad outcome for the British, especially if they failed to inflict serious damage on at least one of their opponents.

He elected to move in with his capital ships in a way that recognised their strengths and weaknesses. Although Prince of Wales had better armour and two more big guns, Holland did not let her lead the attack. His more experienced flagship seemed best suited to direct sustained and accurate fire against Bismarck. As Hood blew up and sank beneath him, while these matters were being put to the test, it became clear that the best intentions of his battle plan had failed.

On the other side of the balance sheet, there was the crucial decision to adopt a steep angle of approach. It was chosen partly to present a more difficult target. With the two enemy ships firing so accurately from the outset, that did not deliver any clear benefit to the British squadron. Holland had underestimated the quality of German gunnery, despite its impressive reputation.

Another doubtful decision was to deploy the British ships in close order, firing only from their forward turrets. These related points also arise: the delay in opening fire, the failure to maximise the use of British heavy guns, and the range being allowed to close as much as it did.

Perhaps by oversight, but consistent with maintaining strict radio silence, Holland did not make any arrangements for the use of lighter forces - destroyers and possibly cruisers - as Hood and Prince of Wales began to close in on the raiders. There was a role for those ships if Bismarck and Prinz Eugen were intercepted, or if they simply decided to turn back.

A spotter 'plane might have been sent from Prince of Wales, to locate the four remaining destroyers and signal them to re-join the attacking force without delay, but it was found to be suffering from contaminated fuel (and later thrown overboard). The interception was limited to a contest between the big guns of capital ships. As an old saying goes, that was like putting all the eggs into one basket.

Weighing Up the Options
A cool examination of the circumstances shows that Holland's chosen course of action was neither an easy one nor arrived at lightly. It can be granted that he weighed up the feasible alternatives. However, his eventual battle plan is certainly open to criticism on points of detail.

The angled approach excluded nearly half of his heavy guns. It may have delayed recognition of the British ships, but failed to protect Hood when she came under fire. It was followed for too long, and those ships did not need to be in close formation while steering for the enemy. When the Germans shifted their attention from Hood to Prince of Wales, that was an aid to target acquisition.

Looking back at those events, making allowance for the complexities and uncertainties of warfare, an engagement on Holland's terms might have succeeded. His one-dimensional 'big ship' solution was not bound to end in disaster. Nevertheless, during that eight minute battle, the execution of his final plan was flawed and his flagship failed to live up to the task demanded of her. Holland overplayed what proved to be a rather weak hand, after losing some of his best cards. Fortune favoured the other side, and the battle of the Denmark Strait had its tragic outcome.

23. Other Matters Arising
Concentration of Forces - Using Destroyers and Cruisers
It is worth noting how Holland failed to concentrate his forces, primarily by not recalling the destroyers from their fruitless search to the north. They were fast, agile and carried torpedoes, which went unused. Two British heavy cruisers were still following the raiders, but as distant spectators. If those ships had been allowed to move in, their 8-inch guns could have been directed against Prinz Eugen. Bismarck might even have been threatened in some measure by the torpedo-carrying HMS Norfolk.

Hood and Prince of Wales were very successful in approaching by stealth, even getting within gunnery range before being identified as capital ships. However, Vice-Admiral Holland's battle plan lacked an important element. He had remained out of radio contact with the destroyers in order not to give away his own presence. Distant by some thirty miles, their support was absent when it was most needed. Failing any other option, as soon as possible after sighting the enemy, and signalling the Admiralty to that effect, he should have recalled the destroyers.

Although they would not have arrived in time to take part in the battle, those ships could have joined forces with Prince of Wales in its aftermath. Destroyers also had the ability to carry out torpedo attacks on Bismarck and Prinz Eugen, as well as shadowing them and acting like a radio beacon to attract other British ships to the area.

With her hull damaged by hits from 14-inch shells, and lacking enough fuel to continue with the mission, Bismarck was already facing a rather uncertain future. Slowed, or possibly immobilised, by torpedoes from the destroyers, a ship in that condition would have been snapped up by the second search force (King George V, Repulse and Victorious).

The Destroyers Get Their Orders

Six destroyers had sailed with Hood and Prince of Wales from Scapa Flow. Of those that lasted the course, it fell to HMS Electra to rescue the flagship's only three survivors. Midshipman W J Dundas, Able Seaman R E Tilburn and Ordinary Signalman A E Briggs spent nearly four hours adrift on small life rafts until they were hauled over her rails, half-frozen and smeared with fuel oil from their sunken ship.

Rear-Admiral W Wake-Walker had become senior officer present. From HMS Norfolk he gave the destroyers their orders to comb the area for survivors. Hours were spent searching, but just those few were found. There was wreckage and oil, but so sudden and complete had been the destruction of HMS Hood that there were not even bodies to recover. On a further sad note, Electra was part of 'Force Z' when HMS Prince of Wales was sunk by Japanese aircraft, and again she picked up oil-covered survivors from the sea.

Hot Pursuit in Arctic Waters

What if the raiders had turned away, on becoming aware that two British capital ships were approaching? The answer is much the same: Holland should have resumed contact with his destroyers. In that case an urgent message was required, ordering them to steer an interception course at full speed towards a now retreating German squadron. Isolated in those unfriendly waters, far from home, with Hood and Prince of Wales in hot pursuit, destroyers and cruisers waiting ahead of them (distantly supported by the second search force), again the future would have been uncertain.

In this alternative version of events, after only a few shots fired, the unexpected appearance of the British squadron brings a sudden end to the German mission. With that much achieved, no damage or casualties on either side, and HMS Hood unharmed, would it have been vital for the raiders to be caught and disabled or sunk? After all, they were no longer a danger to the war convoys.

That question has elements in common with the 'General Belgrano' (Falklands War) controversy of 1982. A clear answer is that it was not a game of half-measures. Bismarck and Prinz Eugen could have tried again, perhaps with greater success on another occasion. In those desperate days, the destruction of enemy warships was a feat of arms expected from the Royal Navy. The escape of Bismarck would have been a deeply negative outcome, a defeat in all but name. As it happens, Prinz Eugen did escape. At least she sank no allied ships, and never did operate as a commerce raider.

The Final Turn to Port
There Is one matter that goes against some accepted wisdom. In print it has been argued that, in executing the final turn to port, Holland was completing the most dangerous part of his approach. HMS Hood was just about to come into her own. A less positive view is that his position was severely compromised.

The two British ships had been taken towards the enemy at an angle of approach where their aft turrets were unable to bear. Hood had begun by firing at Prinz Eugen rather than Bismarck, and had not aimed a single gun effectively at either of them. Damage to the spotting top would have worked against her in shifting target from one to the other. The belated turns to port exposed more of her profile to the full weight of German shells, and the range was still closing.

By that stage the flagship was in serious trouble. She had become a prize target, delivered to the guns of a German battleship and a cruiser. Hood was theirs to hit at will, having lost the ability to fight her ground or even to defend it to best effect. Those factors in combination proved fatal before they could be remedied.

An Immune Zone Revisited
Closing the Range
Given that it was safe for the British flagship to fight at a minimum distance of 18000 yards, and that Vice-Admiral Holland was aware of this limitation, it was not respected during the battle of the Denmark Strait. According to the benchmarks for table 1, the range had decreased to 16500 yards by 0600 hrs. Was the 'safe' distance infringed by accident or by design; if the former, how might it have happened?

A preliminary point is the reliability of the 29920 yard range, reported when the German raiders were first sighted at 0535 hrs. Both British ships had radar. Prince of Wales apparently switched on her gunnery set during the action. However, Vice-Admiral Holland had previously ordered that radar should not be used at long distance, in case its pulses were picked up by the German ships. It was vital that his force should remain undetected for as long as possible.

Some intriguing questions arise. Was that initial range obtained entirely by optical means, without the use of radar? Furthermore, was there a British instrument capable of very high precision when faced with such a distant contact? A tolerance of just 5% could fail to distinguish between 29920 yards (17 miles) and 28424 yards (16.15 miles). Later – who knows – a modest difference of 1500 yards might transform a 'safe' range of 18000 yards into a more dubious one of 16500.

Perhaps Holland was misinformed at the outset. His calculations were affected by an over-estimation of the range, and that error went uncorrected. Not only was the distance between the two squadrons less than he thought, it diminished to an extent he never intended. Alternatively, though a gunnery specialist, perhaps he failed to keep a close watch on how much the range had reduced before the British ships opened fire. Then, in the few minutes after 0552 hrs, he could have been preoccupied with getting the flagship's guns to hit their target.

Maybe he was influenced more by a marine chronometer than a range clock. The British ships were steamed for 12 minutes on course 280 degrees, for the next 8 minutes on course 300, then turned back to 280 degrees for another 3 minutes. When the enemy started to score hits on his flagship, it was time to order a further turn to port. Though begun, this was never completed.

A plausible alternative to any of these is that Holland had in mind a range of 16500 yards, or even 16000, for beginning to fight with 'full broadsides' - and he was determined to get to it, whatever the risks. One way or another there was not enough regard for the likely capabilities of Bismarck's weapons, when deployed against the Hood's defences. Someone on board, in a position of authority, should have been aware of the characteristics of the ship, as to the range or ranges at which she could safely be fought. The alternative to that really does beggar belief.

Applying the Tables
According to the museum journal article, or using the battleship analogue, Hood's immune zone extended for 7000 yards or 9000 yards, relative to an enemy ship comparably armed. That is between about 3.5 and 4.5 nautical miles, which in this case (based on table 1) was covered while the British ships were steaming at 28 knots.

They were turned a total of sixty degrees to starboard, beginning at 0537 hrs, but did not begin to turn back until the better part of twenty minutes later. Range conditions at an early stage were good enough for both ships to have engaged the enemy with the maximum number of big guns. None of those guns began firing until 0552 hrs, and all the while their position was being frittered away. The gunnery range continued to decrease, until finally it reached the generally accepted 16500 yards. Only in the last three minutes of the main action were all the British guns able to bear.

If the results from table 2 are accepted, Hood fired from within an immune zone and remained there until the very last. If the 12-inch belt was sufficient, thanks to a combination of distance from Bismarck and angle of impact, some weaker part or parts of the hull probably failed to resist that final salvo. As explained elsewhere, the data from this table are less dependable than those from table 1.

Table 1 showed that Hood opened fire after passing through the inner limit of a Kemp-sized immune zone of 22500 yards. If German 15-inch shells were capable of piercing the main 12-inch side armour below 18000 yards (using the battleship analogue), when the range reached 16500 yards the ship had also steamed beyond that point. Strictly in zonal terms, either her safety was put at risk by 0554 hrs, when the raiders returned fire, or by 0558 when German shells were beginning to find their mark. On that basis, what the British flagship did was too little, too late and too close.

Side Protection
Hood's X and Y turrets were quite capable of firing forward of the beam, but beyond about 50 degrees there was a serious risk of the quarterdeck and superstructure being damaged by blast from their 15-inch guns. It seems that at least one of those aft turrets began to fire on a starboard bearing as soon as a suitable angle was achieved. Technically speaking, that was when the 'A' arcs opened. It became possible towards the end of the British ships' approach, when Vice-Admiral Holland ordered the first turn of 20 degrees to port.

By then the German squadron had moved ahead. There was also a distinct angle between the raiders and interceptors. Their courses had been converging quite steeply since 0537 hrs. With Bismarck's two aft turrets trained to port (40 degrees is a realistic figure), shells were being fired obliquely towards the Hood. The flagship's sudden end came about while the enemy remained ahead, and before the angle of convergence could be closed. On both counts she was not in a classic broadside position.

Under such conditions, 12-inches of main belt armour should have given more than its minimum level of protection. An outright penetration by a 15-inch (37.5 cm) shell was therefore unlikely, though not impossible.

Above this belt the side armour was thinner, with a maximum of 7 inches and a minimum of 5. If struck at a range of 16500 yards it would not have been equally robust.

Either of these lesser tiers of armour might have permitted the entry of a heavy shell, but inboard of them were protective decks containing a total of five inches of high-tensile steel. Details appear in Appendix D. Those arrangements were reasonably satisfactory, although the armour as a whole was not as well organised as in later capital ships such as Rodney and Nelson, where concentration was chosen as the key to effectiveness.

Deck Protection
According to some long-held views about the loss of the ship, shells from Bismarck's final salvo descended 'at a steep angle' and one of them reached a magazine simply by penetrating Hood's lightly-protected decks. Other research and calculations cast doubt on this. Fired from medium range, those shells were arriving at quite a shallow angle - perhaps no greater than 13 degrees from the horizontal. The question here is how the 4-inch magazine, located about 35 feet down and 25 feet inboard, could have been compromised.

The uppermost (shelter) deck was squarely in the German line of fire. It was not intended to defend the ship against major impacts. Bismarck's final salvo is reported to have scored at least one hit in that area. However, before going deep into the battlecruiser's hull, it needed to overcome the two protective decks, with their five inches of HT steel. A light shell should have exploded or been deflected, causing only local damage, but a heavy one at a steep angle could have passed right through them. Suffice it to say that there had never been complete confidence in the ship's horizontal defences, even with her post-Jutland modifications.

Below these various decks there was a further level of protection, provided by a 2-inch crown shielding the aft magazines. The crown may not have been involved in this case. More than one path was possible for a shell that managed to penetrate so far without exploding. As previously mentioned, the magazines were also shielded by side walls with additional plating 1.5 inches thick.

Aside from the decks and other defensive measures, a major obstacle would have been inherent in the shallow angle of impact. This alone might have kept the shell away from danger areas deep within the hull. Alternatively, as well as a long fuse delay, it would have needed enough momentum to dive down through the decks and travel a serious distance, to reach the 4-inch magazine. A distinctly unfavourable 70 feet does not seem out of the question, although it could have been less (for example, if deflected). All these matters considered, a 'simple' deck penetration turns out to have its own complications.

24. Completing the Picture

The Loss of HMS Hood - Summing Up

There is nothing to suggest that either of the first two incoming salvoes from Bismarck struck the Hood. One apparently fell short, while the other was long. The third has generally been counted as a straddle. There are serious difficulties with making a decisive hit out of the short salvo seen from the compass platform. Of all those that fell, it seems most likely that Bismarck's fifth dealt the British flagship her coup de grace at 0600 hrs.

Taking the immune zone figures for a battleship of the Queen Elizabeth class, and then applying them to this battlecruiser, German 15-inch shells should have been defeated by Hood's main 12-inch side armour at a distance of not less than 18000 yards. The gunnery range was still closing, and had reached about 16500 yards, when the fifth salvo arrived.

Some research on shell performance suggests an angle of descent between 11 and 13 degrees, here combined with a lateral angle of impact of at least 40 degrees. It is not known for certain how many hits were scored, or where. The main belt should have remained proof against a 15-inch penetration; lesser armoured areas of the hull would have been more vulnerable. If a shell avoided all side armour, and struck the shelter deck at a shallow angle, it needed to take a long path within the ship to do serious harm. In its way were two HT steel decks and either a magazine crown or additional protective plating.

There is no obvious connection between the early blaze on Hood's shelter deck and the disaster that was to come, either with or without involvement of a torpedo compartment. Evidence is lacking for a preliminary explosion of some of the above-water torpedoes, from that fire or from a direct hit within Bismarck's fifth salvo. It remains to be shown how such an explosion could have reached the nearest magazine. More probably there was an unrelated cordite fire which ravaged that part of the ship, inflicted widespread structural damage, and quickly sank her.

Hood's back was broken by the powerfully expanding force of that fire, which began in an area containing a 4-inch magazine and the two adjacent main magazines serving X and Y turrets. It first became visible on the shelter deck, then erupted out of the ship's waist, and finally destroyed a large section of the hull. A misfiring gun within X turret is an improbable prelude to this event. According to a German eyewitness, fire reached the main (aft) magazines but did not begin in either of them. In less than five minutes the world's largest ever battlecruiser was gone.

The Main Possibilities
Setting aside less plausible theories, it is most likely that one or more low-trajectory shells from Bismarck's fifth salvo struck towards the rear of the ship, within reach of the four-inch magazine. On that footing, there could have been a fatal penetration by way of Hood's shelter deck, or a shell might have passed over the main armour belt. On balance, it is more likely to have entered below the belt, perhaps after falling slightly short. The prospect of the main belt being pierced can probably be discounted, even though the range had decreased to about 16500 yards.

Before moving on from these matters, one is important enough to deserve elaboration. As Hood began a second turn to port she would have heeled perhaps 5 degrees in that direction. With the starboard side rising higher in the water, and some of the least protected lower parts of the hull becoming more exposed, it was easier for a shell from Bismarck to have struck below her main armour, towards the turn of the bilge.

What area of impact would have offered least resistance - considering the converging course of Hood relative to Bismarck, the horizontal and lateral striking angles of a German heavy shell, plus the location and protection of the aft 4-inch magazine? It can be described thus: a sixty-foot length of hull between her main mast and the step-down from forecastle to quarterdeck, below the main armour belt and just beneath the water line.

That area was adjacent to the turbine rooms. From there the shell needed to travel inboard, roughly on the diagonal, for at least 42 feet and with a commensurate fuse delay. Once inside this thinly-plated part of the hull (0.75" maximum), there was no armour to be defeated. Along with the 1.5" torpedo bulkhead, made of high-tensile steel, there was an assortment of vertical and horizontal surfaces with a combined thickness of about 3.25". This route to the magazine seems the most probable candidate for a 'chink in the armour.' It was revealed to devastating effect when Hood was assailed by the guns of her arch-rival.

How Bismarck Won
Pulling all this material together, it can fairly be said that the destruction of HMS Hood did take place under the impact of battleship Bismarck's accurate gunfire. This had the major benefit of first-class stereoscopic rangefinders, with modern plotting and control equipment operated by a crew recently worked up to

full efficiency. At least one shell from Bismarck probably struck the Hood in such a way that it detonated a 4-inch magazine. Allowing for the proximity of main magazines X and Y, more than ninety tons of cordite charges were there to be ignited. That is quite sufficient to explain why the ship burned so fiercely, then broke apart and sank so rapidly. It was without question a non-survivable event.

Game Over

It was well and truly 'game over' for HMS Hood, one early morning in the arctic waters between Iceland and Greenland. The result could have been different, perhaps if there had been a timely turn to port, ordered before the British squadron opened fire, granted that the flagship still had the benefit of an 'immune zone'. The German ships were already within range and the British had at least seventeen major weapons available. It might have swung that contest the other way.

Instead, there had been a dash to reduce the range, heading straight into the jaws of Bismarck and Prinz Eugen, with a limited number of guns able to fire. Vice-Admiral Holland angled his squadron to starboard and continued to close in until it was too late. He went down with the Hood, along with Captain Kerr and nearly all the others on board. This tragic outcome arose from a time-honoured manoeuvre: the commander turned his ships and engaged more closely with the enemy. Perhaps, like others beforehand, he had in mind the bold tradition of Nelson, whose influence on the British Navy still persisted after so many years.

HMS Hood was given a leading part to play in the interception of two German raiders. Quickly identified as an important capital ship, she became their principal target and suffered total destruction in just a few minutes. Having made no positive contribution to the Battle of the Denmark Strait, despite her 15-inch guns, high speed, adequate armour and a crew of well over a thousand men, it is in order to argue that battlecruiser Hood was not so much 'lost' as 'wasted' on 24 May 1941. As already mentioned, what she did was too little, too late and too close to the enemy.

25. Aftermath
Bismarck, Prinz Eugen and Prince of Wales
Damaged by gunfire and aerial torpedoes, then harried by destroyers, Bismarck was intercepted while vainly trying to reach a suitable port, such as St. Nazaire in occupied France. Unable to steer, and after making an heroic last stand against superior numbers, she was finally neutralised by heavy units of the British fleet.

Battleships Rodney and King George V pounded her with their big guns, and other ships joined in. The cruiser HMS Dorsetshire then delivered a salvo of torpedoes. By this time, battle damage and scuttling charges had reduced the fine German ship to a sinking condition. She rolled over and went down, with heavy loss of life, in the grey Atlantic on 27 May 1941.

HMS Hood had been avenged, but there seems to have been little or no rejoicing over how that had been achieved. Within the British fleet there was admiration for the skill and bravery with which the Bismarck had fought, and sober reflection on how many lives had been lost on both sides. As Admiral Tovey generously put it, Bismarck had put up a most gallant fight against impossible odds, worthy of the old days of the Imperial German Navy, and she went down with her colours flying.

The cruiser Prinz Eugen was fortunate, in not being damaged during the whole episode. Released by Bismarck, to make her own way from the Denmark Strait into the Atlantic, she escaped to the German-occupied port of Brest and went on to survive the Second World War.

Battleship Prince of Wales did not even survive the year. She was operating in far eastern waters, with the older battlecruiser Repulse and several destroyers, when Japanese aircraft attacked their 'Force Z' on 10 December 1941. The big ships were struck by bombs and finally sunk by torpedoes. Of the 1612 men on board Prince of Wales, 1285 were saved.

The Remains of HMS Hood
A well-researched account of the fate of this famous warship can be found in 'Hood - Life and Death of a Battlecruiser' by Roger Chesneau. Of major interest is the final chapter, which concerns an expedition to the Denmark Strait, led by David Mearns in 2001. This located and surveyed the wreck. The story of that expedition is well worth reading in its own right, as contained in the book 'Hood and Bismarck' by Mearns and White.

It has helped to shed light on some important aspects of the dramatic fight to the death between those two powerful ships. Underwater photographs taken during the expedition have demonstrated just how catastrophic was the battle damage suffered by HMS Hood. Not only had she broken in two, as witnessed at the time, but the hull was actually in three main pieces. The dimensions given below are composite figures: sources do not quite agree on the details.

Surveying the Damage
The first 100 feet of her bow section, forward of A and B turrets, had been severed from the remainder of the ship and was resting on its side. Another 345 feet of wreckage - more of the bow section, and the hull as far as the rear of her forward turbine room - was discovered upside down and much damaged. The final piece consisted of 120 feet belonging to the stern section, extending as far forward as the barbette of Y turret,

partly bent upwards and partly resting flat on the sea bottom.

Between the main portion of the hull and the stern section there was nothing. Roughly 230 feet of the ship was missing, from the waist to about the middle of the quarterdeck. It had been dismembered by the force of the blasts that had ravaged the Hood sixty years beforehand.

Gone were two of the three turbine rooms, the torpedo compartments, the 4-inch magazine, X and Y magazines, their turrets and shell rooms. This part of the hull had been shredded, reduced to a confusion of rusting debris deep in the Denmark Strait. Another 65 feet, a section of the bow forward of A barbette, was also missing.

The heavy conning tower was found at some distance from the bulk of the wreckage. If internal fires reached the forward magazine area, further explosions may have helped to scatter the remains of a sinking ship.

One matter of doubt, settled by the Mearns expedition, is that Hood had been making her final turn when disaster struck: the ship's rudder was still angled to port. Not unexpectedly, it has failed to reveal where one or more shells from Bismarck's fifth salvo hit home.

26. Epilogue

The reputation of British battlecruisers waxed and waned, more than any other kind of surface warship, in less than a decade. One of the first, HMS Invincible, began her fighting career on a high note, succeeding in an engagement with a squadron of German raiders. The last ever built, HMS Hood, was found wanting in similar circumstances. Both were suddenly destroyed, in different wars, when faced by stronger opposition. Their names are written into the early and late chapters of the battlecruiser story. Several generations of these fast, graceful ships took an active part - to say the least - in an eventful period of maritime history.

The earliest British battlecruisers were less heavily armoured than their German counterparts. Several of the later ones - Lion, Princess Royal, Queen Mary and Tiger - were more prudently designed in that respect. The Admiralty was prepared to deploy its 'greyhounds' as front-line ships in situations where the defensive features of the older ones were stretched to the limit. Under war conditions the big temptation was to form them into a line, make maximum use of their heavy weapons, and generally treat them as equivalent to fast battleships (which they were not).

Within those ships, rapidity of fire was allowed to take precedence over safe procedures for managing cordite charges and proper anti-flash precautions. This was not evidence that the battlecruiser was a flawed concept, nor did it arise from major faults of design or construction: it was very much to do with the human factor. Dangerous practices were overlooked at the time and the consequences were played down later.

During one major fleet action, three of the British ships exploded and sank while trading blows with German ships. It is at least arguable that two of them need not have done so. Battleship HMS Malaya, one of the Queen Elizabeth class, experienced a serious fire in the 6-inch battery while fighting at Jutland. She was fortunate to have avoided the same fate as battlecruiser Queen Mary. It was not thickness of armour that saved her, but brave action by the crew, taken just in time.

Their German opponents, it should be noted, stood up to a combination of hard hits from the best of British battlecruisers and some of the very latest battleships, when they all came together at Jutland. Excellent fighting ships had been produced for the Kaiser's navy, with better weight distribution in terms of armour versus machinery, hull and armament. They had better rangefinders, shells, and propellant that did not explode when subjected to flash. Their design concept had been well devised, thought through and implemented.

Under combat conditions the German ships out-performed their British counterparts. Only one did not survive the 1914-18 war, in the face of damage from shells, torpedoes and mines, the most powerful weapons current at the time. That overall assessment certainly ticks the boxes. During the rearmament years, leading up to yet another clash of nations, a rejuvenated Reichsmarine took delivery of two new battlecruisers: it was an affirmation of belief in such ships.

The replacement Scharnhorst and Gneisenau, robust fighting machines in any terms, were much respected units of the German navy during the 1939-45 war. Although their 11-inch main armament was less powerful than that of Bismarck and her sister Tirpitz, when used as fast surface raiders there was never any argument that they were unsuitable for purpose by being lightly armed, structurally weak or under-protected. They were not far from being modern, fast battleships. German vessels proved to be all-round capable, and in two major European wars the battlecruisers performed well.

The tragedy of HMS Hood, the last and best of her kind built for the Royal Navy, involved both bad luck and bad judgement. It is fair to say that her protection was weak within the original design, but its major shortcomings had been dealt with by the time Hood entered service.

More than twenty years later, in need of modernisation, she had the misfortune to be pitted against two of Germany's most up to date fighting ships, whose superior gunnery carried the day. Here was a battlecruiser that deserved a better fate and a better press. A battleship of that vintage, thus handled, might have done no better. The circumstances of her difficult birth, glamorous life and sudden death have been examined within this work.

Battlecruiser Hood's final survivor, the late Ted Briggs, visited the Mearns expedition. He helped with the laying of a memorial plaque near the bow section of a much loved ship. There was also a brief service, and a wreath was placed on the cold waters of the Denmark Strait. Hood and Bismarck were sunk within the space of a few hectic days in 1941. They remain united by the deep and timeless sea - two great rivals, both passed into legend.

Appendix A - The Battle of Jutland: Casualties

Killed - British: 6097
Injured - British: 510
Killed - German: 2551
Injured - German: 507

A Selection of Ships Sunk by Magazine Explosions

British (Battle of Jutland, 1916 - 5 ships): 99.5% killed
German (Battle of Jutland, 1916 - 1 ship): 100.0% killed
HMS Vanguard (blew up in Scapa Flow, 1917): 99.7% killed
HMS Hood (sunk in the Denmark Strait, 1941): 99.8% killed
HMS Barham (torpedoed off Sollum, 1941): 68.6% killed

Appendix B - Message from Vice-Admiral Beatty to Admiral Jellicoe, 3 June 1916

"Urgent. Experience of *Lion* indicates that open magazine doors in turrets are very dangerous. Present safety arrangements of flash doors are ineffective when turret armour is penetrated. Flash from shell may reach cordite in main cages and thence to handling rooms. This occurred in *Lion* when turret roof was penetrated, but magazine doors being at once closed saved magazine from catching fire. Almost certain that magazines of three lost battlecruisers exploded from such cause. Consider matter of urgent necessity to alter existing communication between magazine and handling rooms by reverting to original system of handling room supply scuttles, which should be fitted immediately. Meanwhile consider (it) imperative to maintain small stock (of) cordite in handling room for magazine, doors being kept closed with one clip on and opened only for replacement of handling room. Proposed handling room supply scuttles should be capable of being made watertight at will. Commander Dannreuther of *Invincible* will report personally on this matter at Admiralty tomorrow..." ('British Battlecruisers 1914-18' - L Burr. © Osprey Publishing, part of Bloomsbury.)

The Kaiser's navy was ahead in this game. German propellant charges were not immune to flash, but the use of metal cases during the loading sequence meant that fewer of them were vulnerable in that way. Also, turret-magazine safety precautions were tightened up, following the near loss of battlecruiser Seydlitz during the Dogger Bank engagement in 1915. A hit from HMS Lion resulted in a very serious fire which burned out the two aft turrets. Deliberate flooding of their magazines narrowly avoided a complete disaster.

It is central to the Beatty-Jellicoe message that the ammunition supply and magazine safety arrangements within British battlecruisers played an important part in the losses at Jutland. However, it was more convenient for the Admiralty to maintain that their 'lack of armour' was the whole story, and this gained wide acceptance at the time.

Appendix C - Comparison of Percentage of Weights in Tonnes

Ship	Von der Tann	Indefatigable
Hull:	6,004 (31.5%)	7,000 (37.4%)
Machinery:	3,034 (15.9%)	3,655 (19.5%)
Armour & Protection:	5,693 (29.8%)	3,735 (19.9%)
Armament:	2,604 (13.7%)	2,580 (13.8%)
Total:	17,335 Tonnes	16,970 Tonnes

Source: 'German Battlecruisers 1914-18' - G Staff.
© Osprey Publishing, part of Bloomsbury.

Appendix D - HMS Hood: Armour and Other Protection

1. Main Armour
Turrets: 15" (face) 12" (sides) 11" (rear) 5" (roof)
Hull - Main Belt: 12" (angled; thinner at extremities)
Barbettes: 12"
Conning Tower: 11" - 7"
Hull - Middle Belt: 7"
Hull - Upper Belt: 5"
Enclosing Bulkheads: 5" - 4"
Hull - Lower Belt: 3" (main magazine areas)
Funnel Uptakes: 2" – 1.5"
Torpedo Bulkheads: 1.75" - 1.5"

2. Armour Slopes
Between Main Deck and Lower Deck: 2"
Behind Main Belt: 2"
Four Inch Magazines: 1.5"
Between Decks below: 1.5" - 0.75"
Adjacent to Aft Magazines: 0.75"

3. Decks and Horizontal Protective Plating
Main Deck: 3"
Lower Deck, aft: 3" - 1.5"
Magazine Crowns: 2"
Forecastle Deck: 2" - 1.25"
Upper Deck: 2" - 0.75"
Lower Deck, forward: 1.5" - 1"
Total thickness of horizontal protection -
Above Engine and Boiler Rooms: 6.25"
Above Aft Magazines: 6.25 "
Above Forward Magazines: 6"

4. Vertical Protective Plating
Main Magazines: 1.5"
Four Inch Magazines: 1.5"

5. Protection Against Fifteen Inch (37.5 cm) Shells
(Target - Aft Four Inch Magazine – Angled Impact)

Shelter Deck/Magazine: Armour nil; HT Plating 7.75" (best case); Other 1.25" - Total: 9".

Forecastle Deck/Magazine: Armour nil; HT Plating 7" (best case); Other 2.5" - Total: 9.5".

Upper Belt/Magazine: Armour 5"; HT Plating 7"; Other 2.25" - Total: 14.25".

Middle Belt/Magazine: Armour 7"; HT Plating 5"; Other 2" - Total: 14".

Main Belt/Magazine: Armour 12"; HT Plating 2"; Other 3.5" - Total: 17.5".

Below Belt/Magazine: Armour nil; HT Plating 1.5"; Other 4" - Total: 5.5".

Appendix E - An Eyewitness Account - From Prinz Eugen

"As a whole salvo of 15-inch shells from the German flagship reached its target, there was an explosion of quite incredible violence, between the second funnel and the mainmast. The salvo seemed to crush everything under it with irresistible force. Through huge holes opened up in the grey hull, enormous flames leapt up from the depths of the ship, far above the funnels, and blazed for several seconds through an ash-coloured pall of smoke, which spread terrifyingly towards the ship's bows. And this grey mass fringed with red, composed of smoke, fire and steam, was seen to form two billowing columns spreading upwards and outwards, while just below them formed a kind of incandescent dome, whose initial low flat curve rose higher and higher, finally culminating in an explosion of burning debris. The aft magazine blew up, shooting into the air a molten mass the colour of red lead, which then fell back lazily into the sea - it was one of the rear gun turrets that we thus saw rising into the air for several yards. All the inflammable objects in the area at the time - rafts, boats, and deck planking - broke loose, and even as they drifted continued to burn, drawing a thick cloud of smoke over the sea's surface. And in the midst of this raging inferno, a yellow tongue of flame shot out just once more: the forward turrets of Hood had fired one last salvo."
(From 'The Great Ships Pass' by P C Smith.)

Appendix F - **Five salvoes from Bismarck**

How the Salvoes Fell - Revisited
Here it is necessary to look quite carefully at the fall of shot. To clarify the terms used: 'short' means a salvo that fell between Hood and Bismarck; 'long' means one that went over the target and came down beyond her. Where some shells fell short and some long, the salvo counted as a 'straddle'.

From a considered reconstruction of events, the first 15-inch (37.5 cm) gun salvo from Bismarck was fired at 0554 hrs and it was a short, apparently landing some way ahead of the flagship. The range was about 19700 yards, as in the table 1 figures described above. There is no mention of an initial salvo with those characteristics, as seen from the compass platform. This was followed by one that fell long, which is common both to the museum journal article and Ted Briggs. The latter saw distant gun flashes from the German battleship, and he followed the progress of the resulting salvo. The sound of Bismarck's shells passing overhead was reminiscent of an express train. It came down off the Hood's port side, heading away from the ship, so could scarcely have affected any magazine.

Bismarck's third was a straddle, a mixture of short and long. There was also a close short. If our man on the compass platform correctly recalled seeing four high shell splashes to starboard, they did not belong to salvo three. Kemp accepts that the fourth one fell short, making it the Briggs salvo. Number five was on target, and this most probably brought about the rapid destruction of Vice-Admiral Holland's flagship.

In 'HMS Hood: Pride of the Royal Navy', Dr Andrew Norman prefers the salvo which struck the water close to the starboard side. According to this, one of the shells penetrated the 4-inch magazine. There was a jolt. The shell exploded after a very short delay, and detonated the contents. Main magazines X and Y followed suit, very soon afterwards. It is clear that the author has in mind the 4-inch facility adjacent to X magazine - not the equivalent one just aft of B, in a part of the ship visible from the compass platform.

A Distance to Travel

Granted that one salvo from Bismarck was a close short, HMS Hood would have needed to travel between 300 and 600 feet to bring the aft 4-inch magazine up to that area of sea. This allows for the salvo to have landed somewhere along the starboard side visible from the compass platform, but not ahead of the ship. At the British speed of 28 knots, and depending on where the salvo landed, it would have taken between 6.25 and 12.75 seconds for Hood to cover that distance. Table 1 gives a gunnery range of about 18000 yards, at the time of salvo four.

A Long Fuse Delay

The German shells would have been considerably slowed after hitting the water. Being of the armour-piercing variety, the fuses were not intended to explode them immediately on impact. This said, a fuse delay measured in fractions of a second would have been expected: something over 6 seconds seems very long. With shells from Bismarck having an impact velocity approaching 1800 feet per second (1227 mph), in that time an object free to travel through the air could cover more than two miles.

Back to the Compass Platform

Following the arrival of Bismarck's close short salvo, which Ted Briggs observed as four shells crashing into the sea to starboard, and after the occupants of the compass platform had picked themselves up for the first time, the Squadron Gunnery Officer stepped outside. He soon returned and reported that Hood had taken a hit: there was a blaze on the shelter deck. Vice-Admiral Holland then ordered that both of his ships should make a second turn of twenty degrees to port. Meanwhile, the fire should be left to burn out.

The Chief Yeoman of Signals passed that order from compass platform to flag deck, from where the appropriate blue two pennant was hoisted to the yard-arm. Hood began her turn, to enable the range to be closed at a slower rate with X and Y turrets bearing on the enemy. According to Ted Briggs, X turret opened fire but Y stayed silent. Be that as it may, he did not see it happen. Those turrets were well aft, completely invisible from where he stood.

Time Enough

A minute or more had elapsed since Bismarck's four gun salvo splashed down. HMS Hood was damaged, but still in the game. If any of those shells managed to strike her below the waterline, it was not in a critical area. Failing that, their remains would have been heading for the bottom of the Denmark Strait. The aft 4-inch magazine was simply not close enough to have been affected by the fall of shot, which was seen from a position in the forward part of the ship. In any case, another enemy salvo was due. What happened when it arrived has already been described in some detail.

Problems with the Short Salvo Theory

The main events of this battle present problems for the short salvo theory. It allows for a shell from Bismarck to penetrate the 4-inch magazine, and there explode "after a very short delay". What is not explained is how that shell could have lingered in the water while at least 300 feet of the ship passed by. Only then did it manage to penetrate the hull and make its way to the relevant magazine, before finally exploding.

Other difficulties aside, the shell would have needed a very long fuse delay, plus quite extraordinary powers of navigation and penetration. It really does not line up with the salvo seen by Ted Briggs. There is no record of an earlier salvo that fits the case - unless the straddling third was misreported and that was when the 4-inch magazine was compromised. If so, the unstoppable fire that began on board HMS Hood took a couple of minutes to become apparent outside of the hull. That is hard to reconcile with the German account at Appendix E: a salvo - Bismarck's fifth - struck the Hood and a violent explosion then took place.

Notwithstanding the Mearns expedition and its considerable achievements, an exact site for a fatal strike remains obscure. This work proposes "towards the rear of the ship and within

110

reach of the 4-inch magazine", then it narrows the field to "a sixty foot length of hull between the main mast and the step-down from forecastle to quarter deck, under the main armour belt and just below the water line." It is a contribution to the 75 year debate on that subject, arrived at after careful consideration of the various possibilities.

Appendix G - Methodology for Tables 1 & 2

Formulation of the Tables
These examined two possible 'immune zones' - extending down to 22500 or to 18000 yards. According to table 1, HMS Hood had steamed closer than 22500 yards by 0552 hrs and closer than 18000 yards by 0558 hrs. Table 2 places the flagship either marginally within a 'Kemp' zone, or nearly 4700 yards within a 'Queen Elizabeth' zone, at 0600 hrs.

The first table is more broad-brush; it does not include a feature introduced by the second. The latter takes a gunnery range of 25000 yards and explicitly combines it with a time of 0552 hrs. If that coupling is unjustified, and therefore a weakness, it helps table 1 in the plausibility stakes.

Common to both is a straight line plot between two points in time, the first being 0535 hrs. That is linked with an 'official' range of 29920 yds. signalled to the Admiralty from the Denmark Strait. Table 1 simply projects the time forward by 25 minutes to 0600 hrs, where the range (also from sources) is taken to be 16500 yds. Table 2 projects a straight line plot from 0535 to 0552 hrs, with a range of 25000 yds. (as in the museum journal article), and then by extension to 0600 hrs. The table itself gives a final range of 22685 yds.

One minute intervals appear between the given start and finish times. The tables are so arranged that each minute decreases the range by a set amount. It is just below 537 yds./min in the case of table 1 and slightly under 290 yds./min within table 2. (Quick arithmetic: 29920-16500 = 13420; 13420/25 = 536.8 & 29920-22685 = 7235; 7235/25 = 289.4.) Intermediate values can then be read off between 0535 and 0600 hrs, according to the table of choice.

Problems with Sources
This straight line, time-based approach was chosen in the face of problems arising from unrealistic or conflicting battle ranges given in various sources. For example, some claimed that the opening British salvoes were fired at a range of 25000 or even 26500 yds. The disparity between these figures has no clear

explanation. It certainly exceeds the 800 yd. distance between Hood and Prince of Wales in their fighting formation.

Another example is that the British ships were completing an important 20 degree turn to port at about 0557 hrs. This may have occurred at a range of 17000 or possibly 19000 yds. from the German raiders, depending on the source. A disparity of that size does not help to anchor an event to a specific place and time.

Where speed was mentioned in written sources, Hood was stated to have been steaming at her then absolute maximum of 28 knots. The German ships had been making 28 knots, which could have increased to 29 or 30 when they went to action stations. According to some accounts of this battle the raiders exchanged places, with Prinz Eugen reverting to second in line. It is reasonable to assume that the manoeuvre was made in such a way as to avoid disturbing the aim of Bismarck as senior ship. The British carried out some major course alterations, which complicated the plot.

For present purposes, it seemed better to accept the timings of particular events and let the intermediate ranges find their own place in the scheme of things. With only an eight minute period while the Hood's guns were firing, there was less room for uncertainty in that respect. Even then, the latter part of the process was complicated by the unfinished 20 degrees turn to port by the British, during which the flagship was sunk.

Cross-checking
Table 1 uncouples doubtful ranges from events that are easier to locate in time. Table 2 does likewise, but it includes one interim value of 25000 yds. coupled with the time of 0552 hrs. This table calculates the final range at 0600 hrs. Taking eight specific time points within each of the tables, then netting-off the plus and minus ranges (tables compared with published sources) shows that, in aggregate, the sources are more out of step with table 2 than table 1. Some large differences exist within the figures taken as a whole, extending from +6185 yds. down to -4206 yds. Another table is feasible, containing the

113

least possible aggregate difference, but that option has not been pursued because of its doubtful added value.

Lines of Best Fit

It is not claimed that straight line plots are precise tools with which to measure the intermediate battle ranges. Each plot delivers a 'best fit' between the opening and closing points for time and distance. The speed at which the range closed is expressed by the tables in net average terms. In the Denmark Strait, it was less straightforward. Of the four ships involved, the German duo probably kept the steadier course over a 25 minute period. With the enemy in sight, their speed may have been raised to 29 knots. The British ships were steaming hard at a maximum of 28 knots, but their course changed at least three times. Every variation would have had some effect on the rate at which the distance closed, with actual ranges shadowing (but not necessarily matching) the intermediate figures given minute by minute in the tables.

Value of the Tables

Despite that limitation, there is nothing fanciful about the tables. As far as is known, they have no counterpart in other works on this subject. Their plots are a disciplined guide to what was happening during this battle - especially towards the end of it, when the times of key events need to be examined down to the nearest minute and ranges become critical. The tables were cautious about the accuracy of specific ranges given in available sources, and the cross-check carried out did confirm the problems arising from their use.

It is worth mentioning that table 2 did reveal how one set of figures, published elsewhere, deserved to be checked by quite straightforward mathematics. Specifically, if the range closed from 25000 yds. to 16500 yds., during an 8 minute period starting at 0552 hrs, flagship Hood would have been making just over 31 knots. That was above her maximum speed at the time, and it was not even possible in context because the raiders and interceptors were nowhere near to reciprocal courses (i.e. their combined closing speeds could not have approached so high a figure).

114

Ambiguity Remains

The tables have been a valid attempt to examine whether or not HMS Hood engaged the enemy from within an immune zone, for all the uncertainties attached to that subject. They give conflicting results, and each shows the topic in a different light. It is fair to say that table 1 makes the least number of data-based assumptions, and is less favourable to the decision-making of Vice-Admiral Holland when the two squadrons closed and began to engage. The other table clearly falls short of positive proof. Though more favourable to Holland, it throws up a speed anomaly and gives ranges - including the final range - most out of step with all known sources. The accuracy of both tables, it should be said, can never exceed that of the data used to prepare them.

Appendix H - A Theory Examined in Detail

Above-water Torpedo Fittings.
From an early stage in the ship's history there was concern within the Admiralty about the presence of above-water torpedo fittings. Although these weapons might seem misplaced in a warship able to fight at gunnery ranges beyond the ability of any torpedo, fleet commanders believed that they had an important part to play. For example, if a long line of enemy ships happened to come within reach of torpedo attack, it would be a tempting target large enough to hit. The mere approach of torpedoes might make enemy ships carry out sudden manoeuvres, upsetting their formation and their gunnery.

At the beginning of the Hood's career it was argued in favour of the above-water tubes that they were there on an experimental basis, and could be removed at a later date. Contrary to this, by the end of 1927 it had been decided that they should be regarded as war fittings. The armoured box (mantlet) protection was present after a refit of 1929-31. The four tubes, their weapons, some spare bodies, warheads and firing charges thus became a permanent presence on the upper deck.

For more than 20 years the department of the Director of Naval Construction remained of the view that if the above-water torpedoes ever exploded the Hood could be cut in two. The tubes were mounted just above the main strength girders running the length of the ship. When the Admiralty enquired into the loss of HMS Hood, this long-standing concern was given some prominence.

A Torpedo Compartment Explosion.
An examination of this aspect begins with the serious blaze fed by Hood's anti-aircraft rockets and ready-use four-inch shells. About ten tons of those materials had been stored above armour, all of it relatively unprotected. The question is whether fire and explosions affected not just the shelter deck but also the forecastle deck, and then either of the torpedo

116

compartments on the upper deck: a downward spread of perhaps eleven feet.

Storage lockers on the shelter deck would have offered little resistance to the impact of one of Prinz Eugen's eight-inch shells, from which the initial outbreak spread. The Hood was travelling at top speed, so there was more than enough wind to fan the flames from an uncontained fire. Exploding ammunition would rapidly have taken it further, with red hot debris flying in every direction.

Horizontal Protection and the Time Factor
Hood's shelter deck was essentially a load-bearing structure, not as robust as the forecastle deck with its two inches of protective plating. These horizontal surfaces, and an armoured mantlet around the torpedoes at upper deck level, stood in the way of the exploding stocks of ready-use shells and rockets. In the general vicinity of the torpedo compartments were cabins, offices and crew spaces, all with potential to catch fire.

At this point the time factor needs to be recognised. An observer on the German side recorded that the initial shell hit, from Prinz Eugen, took place at 0557 hrs. About three minutes would have been available for events on the shelter deck to do their worst, before complete disaster overtook the ship at 0600 hrs. During this limited time, fire would have had to spread down through the forecastle deck before it could enter an upper deck torpedo compartment.

A Missing Link

Even if it did so, some further link in the chain is needed, to explain the detonation of magazines lower down in the ship. The trail seems to stop short, bearing in mind that the torpedo compartments were quite high up within the hull. The main deck was immediately below, and the middle turbine room was beneath that. A local explosion would have been able to expend its force as follows: laterally at upper deck level; downwards onto the main deck and possibly into the machinery space; upwards through the already damaged

117

forecastle and shelter decks. The nearest magazine was about 70 feet distant, on the far side of the aft turbine room bulkhead, so this steers the debate back to the impact of one or more of Bismarck's fifteen-inch shells.

Appendix I - A Second Theory Examined in Detail

Was that a Misfire?
A curious remark was made during the battle of the Denmark Strait. On board battleship Bismarck, Adalbert Schneider (First Gunnery Officer) was performing his duties within the forward fire control position. Observing his own ship's gunnery, and seeing the target blow up, he was heard to say, "My God, was that a misfire? That really ate into him".

These words, as recollected by Burkard von Mullenheim-Rechberg (Fourth Gunnery Officer), are doubly curious. First, if describing the fall of shot from his own ship, what did Schneider mean by a misfire? An accurate armour-piercing shell, with fuse delay, should explode inside its target. That explosion would be practically invisible at a distance, and the point of impact might show few signs of the event. The term 'misfire' is more appropriate to the performance of a naval gun than a shell. Second, if he had deliberately applied that word to a shell from Bismarck, how could it be said to have eaten into the target? A misfire would imply some kind of technical failure, not a significant strike on the enemy.

A Fresh Perspective
Much serious thought has been given to the proposition that the loss of HMS Hood was attributable to the potency of German gunfire. But there is a less thoroughly examined perspective on her sinking, which recalls the remark from Adalbert Schneider. Could he have been reacting to the consequences of a misfire (his word) by one of the Hood's fifteen-inch guns? In that case, the chief suspect would be a gun from X turret, nearer than any other to the origin of the unstoppable fires that quickly tore through the ship. Perhaps X turret had been blasted from within by an explosion involving the breech of a gun. Did he bear witness to the earliest visible sign of a chain of purely internal events that brought about the destruction of battlecruiser Hood?

Dealing with a Misfire
When a gun literally misfires, it is vital to deal with any materials lodged in the barrel. Failing to do this brings real danger. In the

119

worst case, if the weapon is simply reloaded, it can become double-charged. On being fired again, a shattering blast is highly likely. Misfires have to be detected, and resolved according to a set procedure, to avoid such a serious hazard.

Under normal conditions, the breech of a British 15-inch gun had to withstand a force of some 19 tons per square inch when fired. In the confines of an armoured turret, the effects of a major explosion at the breech end would be devastating both to men and machinery. Events of this kind did occur, and were taken very seriously. Several navies experienced fatal accidents involving both muzzle and breech-loading guns, because of double-charging or where manufacturing defects were revealed.

An additional factor in British ships was the lack of protection for propellant (cordite) charges on their way from the magazines to the guns. Wrapped in fabric and fitted with powder igniters, out of their cases and ready for use, they were vulnerable to a turret fire or explosion. In quantity those charges could act like a fast-acting fuse leading back to the magazine below. The loss of three - nearly four - British battlecruisers during the fighting at Jutland, by way of magazine explosions, has already been mentioned.

The Gunnery Officer's View
How much weight can be attached to the words attributed to Adalbert Schneider? How might the gunnery officer's remark be reconciled with what else is known about the final moments of the British flagship? Importantly, his gunnery-control view of the Hood in action was limited by the angle at which the British ships were approaching. Though clearly able to see the significant effects of a detonation of a main magazine, he could have missed what had begun to show further forward, on the fire-affected shelter deck.

Another Interpretation
On that basis, Hood's four-inch magazine had ignited. The products of this event were bursting into the adjacent turbine room and venting onto the shelter deck. After a very short

interval the inferno penetrated aft, into the main magazines. The progress of this chain reaction, being highly visible, could have prompted Schneider's excited reaction, "My God, was that a misfire? That really ate into him".

Bearing in mind the sequence of events on board HMS Hood, as most commonly reported by eyewitnesses, Bismarck's first gunnery officer was probably mistaken if his diagnosis was a self-inflicted turret 'misfire'. It is more likely that he was reacting to the visible results of fire in the magazines, following one or more hits scored by his own ship.

What Happened to the German Gunnery Officers
Sadly, Adalbert Schneider did not live to put on record any elaboration or qualification of what he said during the heat of battle. Though promptly awarded an iron cross, for the excellent shooting that brought about the destruction of HMS Hood, a few days later he went down with his own ship when she was cornered by other units of the British navy. Burkard von Mullenheim-Rechberg, having survived the sinking of Bismarck, was able to put on record the words he heard spoken.

Appendix J – Recommended Reading

Hood: Life and Death of a Battlecruiser - R Chesneau
Hood and Bismarck - D Mearns and R White
Imperial War Museum Review No. 4 (1989) - Article by P J Kemp
Bismarck and Hood - Great Naval Adversaries - P J Kemp
Flagship Hood - A Coles and T Briggs
HMS Hood: Pride of the Royal Navy - Dr A Norman
Anatomy of the Ship: Battlecruiser Hood - J Roberts
Man O' War No. 6: Hood - M Nothcott
The Mighty Hood - E Bradford
The Great Ships Pass - P C Smith
Battleships - A Preston
The Battleships - I Johnston & R McAuley
The British Battleship 1906 - 1946 - N Friedman
British Battleships of World War One - R A Burt
British Battleships 1914-18 - A Konstam
British & German Battlecruisers - M Cosentino and R Stanglini
British Battlecruisers 1914-18 - L Burr
British Battlecruisers 1939-45 - A Konstam
German Battlecruisers 1914-18 - G Staff
British Battlecruisers of the Second World War – S Backer
British Battleships of World War Two - A Raven and J Roberts
British Warship Design Since 1906 - G M Stephen
Naval Battles of the First World War – G Bennett
The Battle of Jutland - G Bennett
The Battle of Jutland - O Warner
Jutland 1916 - N Steel and P Hart
The Discovery of the Bismarck - R Ballard and R Archbold

Tables 1 & 2
HMS Hood - Battle of the Denmark Strait
Relevance of an Immune Zone (29500 - 22500 or 27000 -18000 yds.)

Table 1 - Rate of Change (Range & Speed) as a Single Line Plot

Times of Events	Distance (yards) between British & German Ships	Rate of Change Yds/Min	Knots	Notes
0535	29920	536.8	15.9	Phase 1 – Visual Contact Made
				Source Distance: 29920 yds
0536	29383	536.8	15.9	Hood has entered a Kemp Immune Zone
				British steering course 240
				Source Distance: 29500 yds
0537	28846	536.8	15.9	Sighting report & 1st course change (40 degrees starboard)
0538	28310	536.8	15.9	Phase 2 – The Angled Approach
0539	27773	536.8	15.9	British ships steering course 280
0540	27236	536.8	15.9	
0541	26699	536.8	15.9	Hood has entered a Queen Elizabeth Immune Zone
0542	26162	536.8	15.9	
0543	25626	536.8	15.9	
0544	25089	536.8	15.9	Source Distance: 28000 yds
0545	24552	536.8	15.9	
0546	24015	536.8	15.9	
0547	23478	536.8	15.9	
0548	22942	536.8	15.9	Hood about to leave a Kemp Immune Zone
				Source Distance: 22500 yds
0549	22405	536.8	15.9	2nd course change (20 degrees starboard)
0550	21868	536.8	15.9	Phase 3 – The Opening Salvoes
0551	21331	536.8	15.9	British ships steering course 300
0552	20794	536.8	15.9	British ships open fire (source time and table distance)
				Source Distance: 25000 yds
0553	20258	536.8	15.9	
0554	19721	536.8	15.9	German ships return fire (source time and table distance)
				Source Distance: 22000 yds
0555	19184	536.8	15.9	Source Distance: 21000 yds
0556	18647	536.8	15.9	3rd course change (20

0557	18110	536.8	15.9	degrees port) Fire on Hood's shelter deck. Hood about to leave a Queen Elizabeth Immune Zone Source Distance: 19000 yds
0558	17574	536.8	15.9	Phase 4 – The Closing Salvoes
0559	17037	536.8	15.9	British ships steering course 280
0600	16500	536.8	15.9	Hood blows up during final course change (20 degrees port) Source Distance: 16500 yds
0601	n/a	n/a	n/a	Hood sinking
0602	n/a	n/a	n/a	Hood sinking
0603	n/a	n/a	n/a	Hood sunk

Table 2 - Rate of Change (Range & Speed) as a Single Line Plot
(including 25000 yds at 0552 hrs)

Times of Events	Distance (yards) between British & German Ships	Rate of Change Yds/Min Knots		Notes
0535	29920	289.4	8.6	Phase 1 – Visual Contact Made
0536	29631	289.4	8.6	Source Distance: 29920 yds Hood has entered a Kemp Immune Zone British steering course 240
0537	29341	289.4	8.6	Source Distance: 29500 yds Sighting report & 1st course change (40 degrees starboard)
0538	29052	289.4	8.6	Phase 2 – The Angled Approach
0539	28762	289.4	8.6	British ships steering course 280
0540	28473	289.4	8.6	
0541	28184	289.4	8.6	
0542	27894	289.4	8.6	
0543	27605	289.4	8.6	
0544	27315	289.4	8.6	Source Distance: 28000 yds
0545	27026	289.4	8.6	
0546	26737	289.4	8.6	Hood has entered a Queen Elizabeth Immune Zone
0547	26447	289.4	8.6	
0548	26158	289.4	8.6	Source Distance: 22500 yds
0549	25868	289.4	8.6	2nd course change (20 degrees starboard)
0550	25579	289.4	8.6	Phase 3 – The Opening Salvoes
0551	25290	289.4	8.6	British ships steering course 300
0552	25000	289.4	8.6	British ships open fire (Kemp time and table distance) Source Distance: 25000 yds
0553	24711	289.4	8.6	
0554	24421	289.4	8.6	German ships return fire (source time and table distance) Source Distance: 22000 yds
0555	24132	289.4	8.6	Source Distance: 21000 yds
0556	23843	289.4	8.6	3rd course change (20 degrees port)
0557	23553	289.4	8.6	Fire on Hood's shelter deck. Source Distance: 19000 yds
0558	23264	289.4	8.6	Phase 4 – The Closing Salvoes

0559	22974	289.4	8.6	Hood still within either Immune Zone British steering course 280
0600	22685	289.4	8.6	Hood blows up during final course change (20 degrees port) Source Distance: 16500 yds
0601	n/a	n/a	n/a	Hood sinking
0602	n/a	n/a	n/a	Hood sinking
0603	n/a	n/a	n/a	Hood sunk

Notes on Tables 1 & 2

1. Tables assume a uniform speed for British ships within each phase (1 knot = 1.152mph).
2. Tables ignore any minor course/speed changes of German ships.
3. Tables show net speed: German ships are moving away.
4. 'Source Distance' indicates a figure from documentary sources.
5. Ranges in second column were calculated by the table as spreadsheet.
6. Course changes 1 & 2 narrowed the British angle of approach and hastened the rate at which gunnery rate closed.
7. Course change 3 widened the British angle of approach and slowed the rate at which gunnery range closed.
8. Course change 4 (incomplete) also intended to slow the rate, with aft turrets able to fire.
9. Hood in Immune Zone (Kemp) between ranges 29500-22500 yds.
10. Hood in Immune Zone (Queen Elizabeth analogue) between ranges 27000-18000 yds.